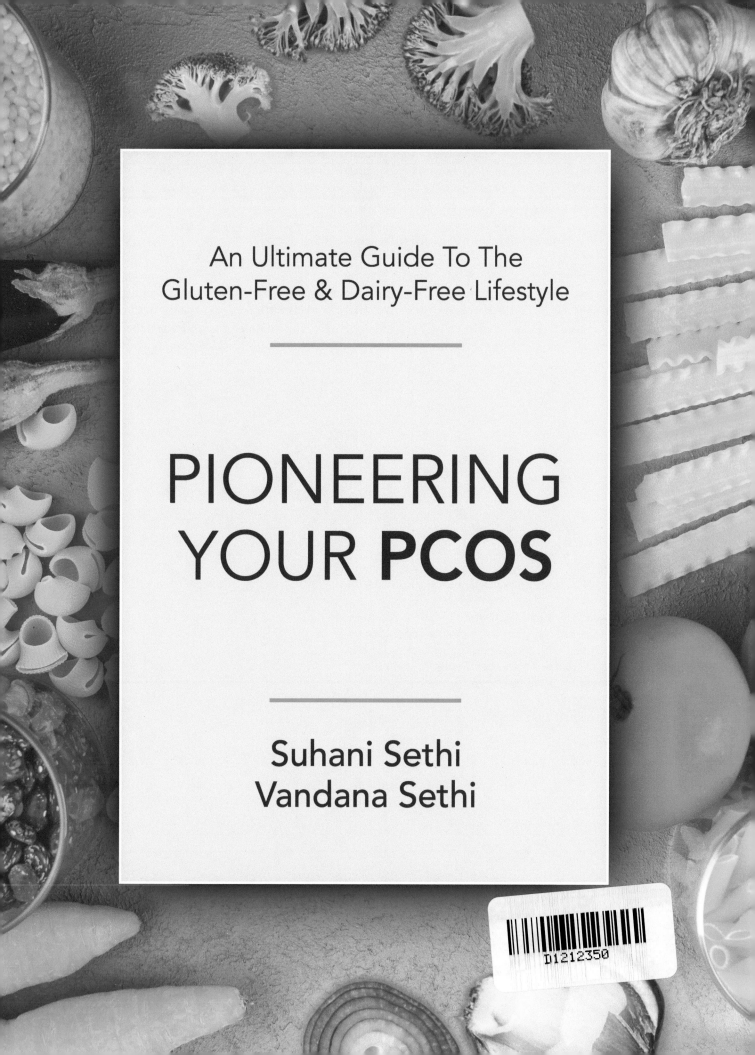

An Ultimate Guide To The
Gluten-Free & Dairy-Free Lifestyle

PIONEERING YOUR **PCOS**

Suhani Sethi
Vandana Sethi

Dedication

In cooking, all dishes are influenced by the ones that come before them. In the same way every new dish has a flavor or technique inspired by another, every great cook is influenced and molded by the people who teach them their craft. While I can not yet claim to be a great cook, I do believe I am on the way to becoming one and for that I have the women I descend from to thank.

To my mom (Vandana Sethi) & grandma (Mrs. Swarn Gakhar)

Thank you for always giving me the best. The high standard of food you have provided all my life has instilled in me high expectations for the food I nourish my body with. The excitement you created around cooking and eating meals together, and the importance you gave to each aspect of preparing the meal sparked my love and passion for cooking. You have been endlessly supportive of my goals, and encouraged me to persevere when I wanted to stop. This book would not have been possible without the countless years of nourishment, both physical and mental, that you both have provided for me.

To order additional copies of this book, contact:
Xlibris
844-714-8691
www.Xlibris.com
Orders@Xlibris.com

Recipes authored by Suhani Sethi, Vandana Sethi
Editors Vandana Sethi, Shareen Sethi
Photography Shareen Sethi
Design Sonali Maniar - Templetree

ISBN: Softcover   978-1-6641-8895-2
        EBook   978-1-6641-8894-5

Print information available on the last page.

Rev. date: 01/11/2022

PIONEERING
your
PCOS

---

*An ultimate guide to
the gluten-free &
dairy-free lifestyle*

Suhani Sethi
Vandana Sethi

About the Author

Suhani Sethi: I have been obsessed with making and eating good food for as long as I can remember. Growing up in an Indian household, lunch conversations revolved around talking about what we would be eating for dinner. Food was a source of happiness, and our meals together as a family bonded us. Family vacations were used as an opportunity to travel and learn about cultures different from our own, but if I am being honest they were mostly an opportunity to try new foods and cuisines.

Unfortunately, the positive connection I felt to food was lost by my Junior year of high school. Suddenly, food became a source of tension and stress rather than comfort and joy, a foe rather than a friend. I felt like the number on the scale was constantly increasing, and my positive body image was suffering. I was determined to lose weight so I adapted my lifestyle. I tried diets, exercise classes, a personal trainer, even a life coach, but none of my efforts showed any results. Eventually, I met with a doctor to figure out if there were any underlying health conditions preventing me from losing weight and feeling healthy. I was diagnosed with Polycystic Ovarian Syndrome (PCOS), a disorder that causes weight gain, acne and bodily exhaustion. I felt even more defeated when I realized this was a disease with no cure. The only way to manage my symptoms was to make major, and permanent, changes to my lifestyle. My diet was the very first change I made.

I made the conscious decision to return to the basics and view food as a tool to nourish my body rather than a source of happiness. After months of research and speaking with medical professionals, I came to the conclusion that I had to cut gluten and dairy out of my diet completely. At first, I couldn't imagine a life without my essentials - bread, cheese, pasta - all the things that taste good. But I knew that I needed to make a radical change in order to feel better, so I did it despite my reservations. Within one week I began to see results. I had found the solution to feeling healthy, now I needed to make it sustainable, and hopefully even enjoyable. My mom and I have spent this lock down time recreating our favorite foods from across the globe - but without any gluten or dairy so that I could genuinely enjoy them even with PCOS.

Now, as a rising senior attending high school in California, I have decided to share my story and the journey I have taken as a 'foodie' with PCOS. After months of experimenting and eating, we have finally curated this cookbook full of recipes that will make your mouth water without negatively impacting your body. I hope that by sharing my story I can support women that suffer from PCOS and help them find their way to nourishment and satisfaction faster than I did.

PCOS may feel like an obstacle that is impossible to overcome, but I promise it is possible to eat good food that will also make your body feel fulfilled and healthy!

Bon appétit.

About the Author

Vandana Sethi: After graduating with a degree in chemistry, I realized that the same process of combining two separate elements to create a new one could easily be applied to creating recipes as well. Since then, I have spent years perfecting my cooking skills and writing my own recipes. I have taught cooking classes in the Philippines, ran a catering business, partnered with local TV channels in India to host cooking shows and co-authored a cookbook with my mother. I have traveled the world, eating my way through many different cultures and cuisines, taking notes along the way and applying them to my own cooking. Sharing my skills and love for food with my children is my greatest joy.

As soon as I became a mother, the health and well being of my children became the number one priority in my life. As my daughters got older, I watched them struggle to find food that did not impact their health negatively. I was heartbroken and worried that they would not be able to share my passion for cooking. We spent months researching, meeting with nutritionists and talking to doctors. After trying medical and holistic remedies, we realized that cutting out gluten and dairy was the best option.

When both of my daughters were officially diagnosed with PCOS, I knew that I needed to find a way to support them as they adjusted their lifestyles to reduce the toll of the food they were eating on their bodies. I have always been a health freak, obsessed with creating well balanced meals that would nourish and fulfill the needs of my children without tasting bland, and yet this was not enough. I realized that I had to majorly change the way we were eating if we were going to manage the impact of PCOS, and despite my extensive background in cooking and food service, I was worried that I would not be able to adjust my cooking to fit the necessary dietary restrictions without losing the delicious food we loved so much. My family has always found comfort and joy in our love for food. Many of our happiest memories were created over shared meals. The dinner table is where we came together, bonded, and shared our lives with one another. We approached this cookbook as a family, determined to continue our tradition of coming together over a delicious home cooked meal.

The COVID-19 quarantine brought my older daughter home, and gave us the opportunity to come together in my kitchen once again. We spent hours curating the recipes in this book, sharing the tears of frustration when we were unable to perfectly recreate a beloved meal, and the immense excitement and pride when we ultimately created something delicious that they could eat without the fear of their bodies reacting badly. This book not only brought us closer, but it proved to us that a dietary change does not have to take away the delicious flavor and delight of eating good food.

Nutritionist Note

Polycystic Ovarian Syndrome (PCOS or PCOD) is a hormonal disorder with no medical cure. It can only be managed by implementing a healthier diet and more active lifestyle. Tackling PCOS is only possible if approached with a positive mindset. Build your self confidence, tell yourself that you can overcome PCOS, commit to a healthy lifestyle and you will achieve your desired results.

As the author says, eliminating dairy and gluten from your daily diet is the best way to reduce the effect of PCOS. This book offers recipes that make going gluten and dairy free appetizing and easy.

You must also stay active. Build daily walks, low cardiac stress exercise, yoga, and meditation into your regular schedule. Give yourself the time and resources you need to feel your best. As often as possible, sleep for eight hours a night, giving your body the opportunity to produce melatonin and rest. This will help your body correct hormonal changes that may otherwise negatively impact you.

If you can adopt and implement healthy lifestyle changes and approach your health from a holistic standpoint you will see positive changes. This recipe book is a fantastic tool to start a path towards feeling better and seeing results.

Sarita Khurana
Nutritionist, Food Writer & Cookery Expert from Zee Khanna Khazana

Nutritionists Tips for Overcoming PCOS

1   Before brushing your teeth in the morning, consume 2-3 glasses of warm water. Drink the water slowly, taking small sips and swallowing completely before taking another sip. Regular water intake in the morning, along with saliva secreted at night, will help fight against acidity in your stomach.

2   If possible, do not consume any coffee or tea throughout the day. Instead, drink coconut water.

3   Soak Methi seeds (Fenugreek seeds) overnight in a glass, and drink it in the morning. Chew the seeds before swallowing.

4   Eat 7-8 soaked almonds and 7-8 shelled walnuts every morning.

5   Start your day with fruit. Some recommendations are apples, pears and any berries.

6   Replace refined cooking oil and vegetable oil with sesame, peanut, coconut, avocado or olive oil for cooking.

7   Cut processed food out of your diet completely. Avoid factory produced foods, instead opting for locally sourced and plant based meals.

8   Steer clear of white sugar. Instead, opt for monk fruit sugar or pure jaggery.

9   Avoid food that has been reheated, especially in the microwave.

10 Dinner should be the lightest meal of the day. Fill your plate with fresh vegetables, fruit and lean meat instead of carbohydrates. When possible, eat dinner before 6pm.

11 Before bed, drink a glass of hot water with cinnamon or dairy-free milk with cinnamon.

12 Add turmeric to your food as often as possible. It will reduce inflammation.

13 Ensure nuts like flax seeds, chia, almond, walnut as some part of your daily intake.

14 Regularly massage your lower legs and the bottom of your feet with oil.

15 Your regular diet should consist of gluten-free and dairy-free foods, lean protein, high fiber vegetables, and anti-inflammatory food and spices.

16 Allow your body to reach a happy balance. Do not overeat or undereat. Exercise regularly but do not overexert your body. A balanced lifestyle will lead to balanced hormones!

Pantry Essentials for Cooking with PCOS

I suggest that you stock the pantry with these essential ingredients and always have them on hand. This ingredient list is a fantastic place to start, but it is not comprehensive so make sure to check the specific ingredient list for your desired recipe.

OILS

- coconut oil butter flavour
- avocado oil
- olive oil
- peanut oil
- sesame oil

DAIRY-FREE YOGURT

- cashew yogurt
- almond yogurt
- coconut milk yogurt

SAUCES

- gluten-free soy sauce (tamari)
- teriyaki flavored coconut aminos
- coconut aminos
- garlic sauce

SWEETENERS

- monk fruit sweetener
- jaggery

SPICES

- turmeric
- tajin
- lemon pepper
- garlic salt
- garlic powder
- onion powder
- red chilli powder
- cream of tartar
- cumin powder (jeera powder)
- coriander powder (dhaniya powder)
- dry mango (amchur powder)

FLOUR

- tapioca flour
- rice flour
- cornstarch
- gluten-free multigrain atta
- buckwheat flour
- oat flour
- millet flour
- potato starch
- amaranth

Acknowledgements

First and foremost, I would like to thank my sister (Shareen Sethi) for being such a great partner and support system as I embarked on my health journey. You were always there to lift me up and motivate me when I felt discouraged. Without your push to pursue my goal of completing a cookbook, this project would have been impossible. Without your amazing photography skills, I would not have been able to capture the beauty of these dishes. Thank you for all you have done.

I would also like to thank my step father (Rohit Tandon) for maintaining a positive attitude through this shift in lifestyle that you did not necessarily want or need. Even when we forced you to be our guinea pig, trying all of our new gluten and dairy-free (and sometimes even meat free) recipes you continued to be supportive. Thank you for your understanding and your cooperation!

Last but definitely not least, my deepest gratitude to my sister's friend Rachel Gärlick. Thank you for spending countless hours helping me edit and curate my recipes into something that is presentable and easy to comprehend. Thank you for constantly giving me suggestions and guiding me towards being a better writer, always lending a helping hand and dealing with all the last minute changes we were constantly making - this book would truly be incomplete without you.

Contents

Contents

Contents

KOREAN

1 Defrost the edamame in a steamer or microwave.

2 In a medium pan heat the chilli oil. Add the garlic and saute over medium heat for 1 minute or until the garlic gets a light brown color and turns aromatic.

3 Add the chilli paste and cook for 30 seconds more. Add the gluten-free soy sauce. Remove from heat and cool.

4 In a medium bowl mix the mayonnaise, lemon juice and the above cooled mixture. Add the warm edamame and stir until coated. Serve.

AUTHORS TIP
• You can also defrost the edamame by cooking in salted boiling water for 5 minutes, or until tender.

Edamame in spicy garlic sauce

Prep time: 10 mins
Cook time: 20 mins
Serves: 4

3 cup frozen edamame
4 garlic cloves, minced
½ tsp chilli oil
½ tsp chilli paste
1 tsp mayonnaise
1 ½ tsp gluten-free soy sauce
1 tbsp lemon juice
Salt to taste

JapChae

Prep time: 10 mins • Cook time: 15 mins
Serves: 3

3 cloves garlic
2 cups white mushrooms, thinly sliced
1 large carrot, julienned
½ large onion, sliced
1 red bell pepper, julienned
1 box korean glass noodles
2 tbsp sesame oil for marination
1 tbsp sesame seeds
½ - 1 tsp cayenne pepper
3 tbsp gluten-free soy sauce
1 tsp sesame oil for cooking

1   Cook glass noodles according to the instructions on the packaging. Once cooked, drain the water and run the noodles under cold water until cool. Move to a large bowl and set aside.

2   Add onions, carrots and mushrooms and bell pepper to the noodles.

3   In a separate bowl, mix together sesame oil, garlic and gluten-free soy sauce. Add cayenne pepper or chili flakes to reach desired spice.

4   Pour the sauce over the noodles and vegetables. Cover and marinate in the fridge for 2-3 hours.

5   Heat a pan over medium-high heat and lightly coat with sesame oil. Add the marinated noodles and cook for 4-5 minutes, stirring occasionally. Add chopped bok choy and cook for another 3-4 minutes. When the noodles are cooked all the way through, garnish with sesame seeds and serve.

AUTHORS TIP
•   Shirake noodles have a similar texture to Korean glass noodles and make a fantastic healthier alternative!

Spicy Bulgogi Pork

Prep time: 10 mins
Cook time: 20 mins Serves: 4

3 cloves garlic
2 ½ inch ginger, cubed
2 tbsp gluten-free soy sauce
1 tbsp red chili flakes
½ tsp red chili powder
2 tbsp sesame oil
2 tbsp oil
1 sweet apple or pear, sliced
3 pounds pork belly or pork
shoulder, sliced across the
grain to get thin slices
1 large yellow onion, thinly sliced
2 tbsp sesame seeds
2 stalks green onions, finely
chopped

1 In a food processor grind garlic, ginger, soy sauce, sesame oil, chili flakes, chili powder, oil, and apple / pear until a thick paste is formed.

2 In a large bowl add the pork, onions and apple paste. Mix until fully combined. Cover and let it marinate anywhere from 2 hours to 2 days.

3 To prevent meat from sticking, pre-heat a large pan or skillet over medium heat and if desired, coat lightly with oil. Add the marinated meat to the pan and cook over high heat for fifteen minutes. Reduce heat to medium, add 2-3 tablespoons of water and cover the pan. Let cook for 6-7 minutes, allowing the pork to become soft and slightly steamed.

4 When the pork is almost cooked through, uncover and cook on high again until it has reached the desired char. To achieve a smokier bulgogi flavor, cook the pork until blackish in color. Once the pork has reached desired char, move it to a large bowl and garnish with green onions and **sesame seeds.**

5 Serve with boiled rice.

Kimchi Pancakes

Prep time: 10 mins • Cook time: 7 mins
Makes 5-7 pancakes

2 cups of homemade or store bought kimchi
1 tsp olive oil / avocado oil
½ large white onion, thinly sliced
2 cloves of garlic, grated
1 tbsp sesame
2 tsp sesame seeds
1 tsp red chili flakes
½ - 1 tsp cayenne pepper
¾ cup rice flour
½ cornstarch or arrowroot powder

1   Chop kimchi into small pieces, approximately half an inch each. Keep and set aside any liquid left over from the kimchi.

2   In a large bowl, whisk the sesame oil, garlic, sesame seeds, cayenne pepper, red chili powder and remaining kimchi juice until combined. Add the cornstarch and rice flour to the mixture and stir until thick. The mixture should be thick enough to remain on the back of a metal spoon after removing. Add water or rice flour to reach desired consistency.

3   Add the chopped kimchi and onions, mixing until they are coated in the flour mixture.

4   Over medium heat, coat a pan lightly with oil and enough batter to form a half centimeter thick evenly spread pancake.

5   Cover the pan and let the pancake cook on medium heat for approximately 4 minutes until crispy . Reduce heat to low and cook the pancake for 2 more minutes.

6   Flip the pancake and cook for 3-4 minutes. Garnish with green onions and sesame seeds and serve immediately.

Kimchi Fried Rice

Prep time: 10 mins
Cook time: 15 mins
Serves: 4

1 ½ cups carrots, shredded
½ cup peas, defrost if frozen
1 small red bell pepper, chopped
1 small yellow onion, chopped
4 scallion stocks, chopped
2-3 cloves garlic, minced
2 cups brown rice, boiled
1 cup store-bought kimchi, chopped
1 tsp sesame seeds, toasted
2-3 eggs
2 tbsp sriracha sauce
3 tbsp sesame oil
2 tbsp gluten-free soy sauce

1   In a large wok heat 2 tbsp oil. Add the onions and sauté until transparent. Add garlic and sauté for another minute.

2   Add the carrots, bell pepper and peas. Cook until the vegetables become tender. Add the scallions and cook until soft.

3   Roughly chop the kimchi and sauté until it begins to turn translucent. Save the remaining liquid from the kimchi.

4   Add the cooked rice, soy sauce and leftover liquid from the kimchi. Mix well.

5   In a small bowl, whisk the eggs. Add sriracha sauce and sesame oil.

6   Move the rice to the sides of the wok creating a hole in the middle. Pour the egg mixture into the hole, scramble and mix with the rice until combined.

7   Top with sesame seeds and green onions and serve!

THAI

Chicken Satay
with Peanut Sauce

Prep time: 5 mins • Cook time: 30 mins • Serves: 6

1 In a medium bowl whisk all of the ingredients for the marinade together.

2 Cut the chicken into bite size pieces. In a shallow dish, place the chicken and cover with the marinade. Stir to combine and refrigerate overnight or for at least 2 hours.

3 In a food processor grind the peanuts until they become a rough powder. In a large pan, sauté the garlic until light brown. Reduce the heat to medium-low and add the red chili powder and ½ cup coconut milk.

4 Bring to a boil, and stir continuously for 3 minutes. Add the crushed peanuts, monk fruit sugar, apple cider vinegar, tamari sauce and lemon pepper. Let simmer for 3-4 minutes.

5 Add the remaining coconut milk and bring to a boil. Reduce heat to low and cook for 4 minutes, stirring constantly. Transfer to a bowl and cool completely. The peanut sauce is ready.

6 Lightly soak the bamboo skewers and skewer the chicken. Preheat the grill to 375°F and spray generously with oil. Grill the chicken skewers for approximately 3-4 minutes on each side. If the chicken becomes dry. Add more marinade while it grills.

7 Serve with peanut sauce!

1 lb boneless chicken
8 bamboo skewers

MARINADE
2 tsp avocado or olive oil
3-4 tbsp coconut milk
1 tbsp lemon juice
2 tsp gluten-free soy sauce
2 tsp crushed garlic
1 ½ tsp cumin powder
1 ½ tsp coriander powder
1 tsp lemon pepper
¾ tsp red chilli powder
2 tsp monk fruit sugar sweetener
1 tsp salt

PEANUT SAUCE
¼ cup roasted salted peanuts
1 tsp coconut oil
¾ tsp garlic, crushed
½ tsp red chilli powder
½ tsp monk fruit sugar sweetener
2 tsp apple cider vinegar
1 tsp gluten-free soy sauce (Tamari)
1 cup coconut milk

Black Mushroom & Cabbage Stir Fry

Prep time: 25 mins
Cook time: 15 mins
Serves: 2-3

8-10 garlic cloves, chopped into two
1 white onion, largely chopped into shells
8-10 cremini mushrooms, de-stemmed and cut in halves
2 cups napa cabbage, shredded into large chunks
2 tsp fish sauce
2 tbsp gluten-free soy sauce
2 tsp rice wine vinegar
1 ½ tsp cornstarch or cornflour
2 tbsp avocado or olive oil
½ tsp lemon pepper
5-6 dried red chili
Salt to taste

1 In a wok, heat oil and add half of the garlic to sauté. After 1 minute, add the onion and sauté until translucent. Add the remaining garlic and red chili pepper to the wok.

2 Increase the heat to high, add the mushrooms and cook until tender.

3 Add the cabbage, soy sauce, rice wine vinegar, fish sauce and lemon pepper. Cook for 2-3 minutes.

4 In a small bowl, mix the cornstarch with 4-5 tbsn water until a thick paste is formed. Add to the wok mixture and cook until fully mixed at high heat.

5 Serve with garlic rice or lemon-grass quinoa!

Lemon Noodles

Prep time: 7-10 mins Cook time: 15 mins Serves: 4

8-10 ounces Saifun bean thread noodles
1 cup carrots, thinly sliced
1 cup sayote, thinly sliced
12-14 curry leaves
3 green chillies, deseeded
& chopped long
1 tsp cumin seeds
1 ½ tsp mustard seed
1 tsp turmeric
¼ tsp lemon pepper
¼ tsp cream of tartar powder
4 tbsp fresh lemon juice
2 tsp urad dal (split black gram) Cilantro
for garnishing
Salt to taste

1 Cook the glass noodles according to the directions on the packaging. Drain and rinse the noodles in cold water until completely cooled.

2 In a large pan, heat oil over medium heat. Roast the cumin seeds, mustard seeds, urad dal and curry leaves, stirring often, until aromatic.

3 Add the carrots and the sayote to the pan. Cook until soft. Add turmeric, lemon pepper, cream of tarter and salt.

4 Mix the glass noodles into the pan. Add the lemon juice and chili, stirring until combined. Cook the noodles for approximately 3-4 minutes.

5 Garnish with cilantro and serve immediately.

AUTHORS TIP
• Add coarsely ground peanuts as garnish for extra flavor and texture.

Chickpea & Kale Coconut Curry

Prep time: 5 mins • Cook time: 15 mins
Serves: 4-5

1 large white onion, diced small
2 tbsp lemongrass paste
2 tsp ground galangal (thai ginger)
3-5 kaffir lime leaves
5 cloves garlic, finely chopped
2 cups chickpeas
4 cups water, chicken broth or vegetable broth
2 ½ cups coconut milk
4 tbsp red curry paste
1 cup carrots, shredded
2 cups baby kale, chopped
2 tsp lemon juice
1 tsp fish sauce
½ - 1 cup chicken broth
½ tsp lemon pepper
½ tsp red chilli powder
2-3 tbsp coconut oil (butter flavor)
Salt to taste
Basil to garnish

1 Heat the coconut oil on medium high in a deep pot. Add the onions and sauté until translucent. Add the galagal, garlic and lemongrass paste. Cook for 3-4 minutes, then add the red chili powder. Cook for another 1-2 minutes, or until fragrant.

2 Add the red curry paste, chickpeas, coconut milk and carrots. If desired, add the fish sauce as well. Bring the mixture to a boil. If the sauce is too thick, add broth. Reduce the heat and add the torn kale, lemon pepper and salt. Cover the pot with a lid and cook until the kale is tender.

3 Throw in the kaffir leaves, lemon juice and basil leaves, stirring until combined. Serve with boiled quinoa or brown rice.

Spicy Thai Dragon Balls

Prep time: 15 mins
Cook time: 12-15 mins
Serves: 6

1 pound minced chicken
4 tbsp lemongrass paste
1 ½ tbsp grated galangal
(thai ginger)
1 tbsp green curry paste
2 tsp fish sauce
10 green beans, finely chopped
1 large red chilli pepper,
finely chopped
½ cup onion, diced
2 tbsp rice flour
2 tbsp coriander, chopped
2 tablespoons lemon juice
¼ tsp red chilli powder
Salt to taste

1   In a large bowl toss the pork with the lemon grass paste, galangal, fish sauce, red curry paste, red chili powder, salt and lemon juice. Mix until the chicken is fully coated.

2   Add the beans, onions, and coriander leaves. Mix until combined. Add the rice flour and mix well.

3   Divide the pork mixture into 20 portions. Roll each portion into a ball and place on a lined baking sheet.

4   Place in the oven at 400°F for 20 mins. Flip the tray around half way through for an even cook.

5   Serve with thai chili sauce and lettuce.

AUTHORS TIP
•   Alternatively, you can use red or yellow curry paste for a different flavor.

Lemongrass Quinoa

Prep time: 5 mins • Cook time: 30 mins • Serves: 3-4

6 cloves garlic
1 ½ tbsp lemongrass paste
1 tsp thai ginger (galangal),
finely chopped
2-3 kaffir lime leaves, roughly chopped
1 large white onion, finely chopped
1 tbsp coconut milk
¾ cup quinoa
1 ½ cup chicken broth
2 tbsp avocado oil or olive oil
1 tbsp lemon pepper
¼ tsp garlic salt

1 Rinse the quinoa. In a small saucepan, add the quinoa and chicken broth and bring to a boil. Reduce the heat, cover the pot and let simmer for approximately 15 minutes, until the broth is completely absorbed. Remove the quinoa from heat and set the covered pot aside. After 5 minutes, fluff the quinoa with a fork.

2 In a wok, heat the oil over medium high. Add the garlic, lemongrass paste and thai ginger. Sauté for 1 minute then add the onion. Continue to sauté until the onion is golden brown.

3 Add the kaffir lime leaves, lemon pepper and garlic salt. Stir in the quinoa and lightly toss, sprinkling the coconut milk over the rice mixture and mix well before serving.

Thai Chicken Sticky Rice

Prep time: 15 mins
Cook time: 40 mins
Serves: 3-4

1 cup rice
1 red bell pepper, cut into thin strips
1 green bell pepper, cut into thin strips
1 yellow bell pepper, cut into thin strips
1 white onion, thinly sliced
½ cup carrots, shredded
1 ½ lb organic chicken breast
1 ½ tbsp of olive oil

FOR THE SAUCE
¼ cup gluten-free soy sauce
2 tbsp apple cider vinegar
1 tsp monk sugar sweetener
1 tsp galangal, finely chopped
2 kaffir lime leaves
4 green onions,
cut into long thin strips
½ tsp gluten-free red chilli paste
Pinch of red pepper flakes
Basil to garnish

1   In a large pot, add the chicken and enough water to fully cover it. Salt the water slightly. Cover and bring to a boil. When the water is boiling, reduce the heat to low and simmer for an additional 25 minutes until the chicken is cooked through.

2   In another pot, add 1 ½ cups of water and the rice to cook. Bring to a boil, then reduce heat to low. Cover and cook for 18-22 minutes.

3   When the chicken is cooked through, remove from the pot and set aside to cool. Using a fork, shred the chicken. In another pan, heat 1 tsp oil and saute the chicken until it becomes just a little golden. Set aside and cool.

4   In a large skillet, add the olive oil and sauté the onions on medium high for 3-4 minutes. Add the bell pepper and sauté for another 5 minutes. Add the carrots and sauté until the onions and pepper are caramelized. Add kaffir leaves and remove the pan from heat.

5   In a small pot mix all of the necessary ingredients for the sauce except for the green onions. Bring the sauce to a boil, adding chili or salt to adjust to desired flavor.

6   Mix the sautéed vegetables, chicken and rice until fully combined. Over medium heat add the sauce to the rice mixture and stir the ingredients together.

7   Garnish with green onions & basil.

Bok Choy Noodle Salad

Prep time: 15 mins • Cook time: 5 mins • Serves: 4

2 ½ tsp gluten-free soy sauce or coconut aminos
2 ½ tsp rice wine vinegar
1 tbsp of ginger garlic paste
1 tsp of coconut sugar or jaggery
2 tbsp avocado oil or sesame oil
½ cup gluten-free millet
& rice ramen noodles
1 ¼ cup bok choy
¼ cup slivered almonds
1 tbsp white roasted sesame seeds
1 tbsp black roasted sesame seeds
Garlic salt to taste
Oil for frying

1   In a deep pot, heat oil over medium-high heat. Break the ramen noodles into small bunches and place in the oil one by one. They will expand quickly and double in size. Take them out of the oil when they become crisp and place on a paper towel to soak up the excess oil.

2   In a glass mason jar, mix the gluten free soy sauce, rice wine vinegar, ginger garlic paste, coconut sugar and 1-2 tablespoons of oil and garlic salt. Tightly screw the lid onto the jar and shake vigorously for 1-2 minutes. The dressing is ready.

3   Tear the bok choy leaves roughly off the stem and cut the bottom into bite size pieces.In a large bowl, add your bok choy, slivered almonds and sesame seeds.

4   Just before serving, pour the dressing on the bok choy bowl and toss well. Add the crispy noodles and mix once again and serve immediately.

AUTHORS TIP
•   Incase you are using coconut aminos teriyaki soy then add less sugar because it is already sweet.

CHINESE

Chicken & Bamboo Shoot Lettuce Cups

Prep time: 15 mins • Cook time: 20 mins • Serves: 5

1.5 pounds of skinless, boneless chicken
thighs cut into
½ inch pieces
8-10 leaves of romaine lettuce
1 cup canned bamboo shoot, chopped
¾ cup red & orange
bell pepper, chopped
1 tbsp peanut butter
1 small white onion,
finely chopped
3-4 garlic cloves, finely sliced
2 green spring onion
1 ½ tbsp rice wine vinegar
1 tbsp avocado oil
1 tbsp sesame oil
2 tsp chilli oil
5 drops of Tabasco hot sauce
2 tsp gluten-free soya sauce
¼ tsp garlic salt
¼ tsp lemon pepper
1 tsp cornflour
4 tbsp chicken broth

1   In a medium bowl combine the peanut butter, gluten-free soy sauce, and rice wine vinegar. Add the chopped chicken and toss until fully coated, cover and put in the refrigerator to marinade for at least an hour.

2   In a wok, heat the avocado and sesame oil over medium heat. Add the garlic and sauté until golden. Increase the heat to high, add the white onion and saute for 3-4 minutes more. Add the chili oil and bamboo shoots, and cook for 2-3 minutes.

3   Add the marinated chicken to the wok and stir fry on high until the chicken is cooked through. Add the garlic salt & lemon pepper and stir. Stir in the bell peppers and Tabasco until fully mixed.

4   In a separate bowl mix the cornflour and chicken broth. Add to the wok and increase the heat to high. Sauté for 1-2 minutes until combined. Add the spring onions and mix well.

5   Cut the lettuce horizontally, creating little cups. Spoon the chicken mixture onto the lettuce bowls and garnish with the leftover greens. Serve immediately.

AUTHORS TIP
•   If desired, garnish with fried glass noodles for an extra crunch.

Spicy Fish Fillet with Bok Choy

Prep time: 5 mins
Cook time: 10 mins
Serves: 4

1.5 pounds swai basa fish fillet
10-12 cloves garlic, thinly sliced
1 inch piece fresh ginger, thinly sliced
1 tbsp sesame oil
1 tbsp chilli oil
2 tbsp dairy-free butter
4-5 thai red chillies, chopped
½ tsp lemon pepper
Salt to taste

FOR THE BOK CHOY
1 pound baby bok choy
1 ½ tsp sesame oil
1 tsp dairy free butter
4-5 garlic cloves, finely chopped
¼ tsp chilli flakes
2 tbsp fresh lemon juice
Garlic salt

1   Rinse the fish fillet and blot dry with a paper towel. Season with salt and lemon pepper.

2   Mix the chili oil with the sesame oil & butter. In a shallow pan, add 2 tbsp of the mixture and heat. Add the garlic and the ginger. Sauté until the garlic becomes golden. Add the fish filet, cooking each side for approximately 3-4 minutes, adjusting the time according to the thickness of the fillet.

3   After flipping the fish, ladle the garlic, ginger & butter over the fillet using a spoon. Add the chillies on the side of the pan, next to the fish, and drizzle them with oil to roast

4   Wash and clean the bok choy leaves well, and cut them in half. Heat the oil and the butter in a large wok and add the garlic. Just before the garlic becomes golden, add the chili flakes.

5   Add the bok choy to the wok, placing them evenly across the bottom of the pan. Sprinkle the bok choy with garlic salt and cook over medium heat for 2 minutes. Flip and cook the other side for 2 minutes more. When the leaves are wilted and the bottom is soft, remove the bok choy from heat. Sprinkle the leaves with lemon juice and serve with the fish.

Chinese Chicken Salad

Prep time: 20 mins • Cook time: 5-7 mins
Serves: 4

4 ounces bean thread noodles
1 head lettuce, shredded to approx 2 ½ cups
3-4 green onions, diagonally sliced thin
3 tbsp slivered almonds
1 ½ tbsp toasted sesame seeds
¼ cup cilantro, chopped
1 large chicken breast
Oil for frying

FOR THE DRESSING
5 tbsp rice wine vinegar
2 ½ tbsp olive oil or gluten-free salad oil
2 tbsp sesame oil
1 tbsp gluten-free soy sauce
¾ tsp lemon pepper
1 tsp black pepper
2 ½ tbsp monk sugar
Salt to taste

1 In a large pot cover the chicken with lightly salted water. Cover and bring to a boil.

2 Reduce the heat to low and simmer for 25 minutes, or until the chicken is cooked through.

3 Remove the chicken from the pot and set aside to cool. Shred the chicken.

4 Whisk together the rice wine vinegar, olive oil, sesame oil and gluten-free soy sauce. Add the sugar, salt, black pepper and lemon pepper. Mix until combined. Let the dressing sit for 30-45 minutes until the flavors are blended. Do not leave out for more than 45 minutes or the dressing will become too thick.

5 Heat 1 cup olive oil in a large wok and heat to 350°F. Add the noodles. They will quickly double in size. Flip the noodles and cook on the other side for a few seconds. Remove from the oil and place on a paper towel to drain the oil.

6 Using the same oiled wok, fry the slivered almonds until they begin to become golden. Do not overcook the almonds, or they will become bitter.

7 Just before serving, put the lettuce in a large salad bowl with the spring onions, cilantro, shredded chicken, slivered almonds and sesame seeds. Pour 2/3 of the dressing over the salad and toss.

8 Add the crispy noodles and gently mix. Serve immediately.

AUTHORS TIP
• The recipe purposefully makes more dressing than necessary to be added on individual plates if desired.

Spicy Green Beans & Pork

Prep time: 15 mins • Cook time: 30 mins • Serves: 3

FOR THE BEANS
½ pound green beans, trimmed
2 tbsp chilli oil
1 ½ tbsp ginger-garlic paste
1 tbsp garlic, thinly sliced
1 tbsp chilli paste
2 tbsp gluten-free soy sauce
1 tbsp rice wine vinegar Pinch of lemon pepper Pinch of monk fruit sugar Garlic salt to taste

FOR THE PORK
1 pound minced pork
4-5 cloves garlic, thinly sliced
2 tsp cornstarch
1 tsp rice wine vinegar
1 tsp coconut amino gluten-free garlic sauce
2 tbsp gluten-free soy sauce
1 tsp gluten-free teriyaki sauce
5-6 dry red chillies
2 tbsp chilli oil

FOR THE BEANS
1   Heat the chili oil in a wok over medium heat. Wash the beans and add them to the wok while they are still wet. Do not stir the beans while they cook for 2 minutes. Toss the beans and cook for 2 more minutes.

2   Add the garlic, chili paste, and garlic-ginger paste to the wok and stir constantly until the beans begin to shrivel.

FOR THE PORK
3   In a large bowl, mix the cornstarch, garlic sauce, gluten-free soy sauce, teriyaki sauce, and rice wine vinegar until combined. Add the pork and use your hands to coat the pork in the sauce.

4   Cut the red chili diagonally into bite size pieces.

5   In a wok, heat the chili oil over medium high heat. Add the garlic and saute until it begins to turn golden. Add the pork and saute for 7-8 minutes, or until it begins to brown.

6   Add the dry red chilis and the cooked beans. Mix well and serve with ramen noodles or rice.

MAKING CHILI OIL
1   Heat 1 cup avocado oil or olive oil over medium low heat. Add 1 tbsp sichuan peppercorn, 2 star anise, and 1 black cardamom. Bring to a boil and let cook for 5 minutes over a low flame.

2   In a separate jar, add 3 tbsp of coarsely ground chili powder and ½ tbsp salt.

3   Pour the peppercorn mixture into the jar and mix. Let the oil sit for a few days before using to let the flavor marinate.

Pan Fried Noodles & Tofu

Prep time: 25 mins
Cook time: 15 mins
Serves: 4

3 cups boiled noodles
3 tbsp avocado oil

FOR THE VEGETABLES
½ cup thinly cut green beans
½ cup brussel sprouts, thinly sliced
½ cup red or orange bell pepper, chopped
½ cup bamboo shoot
½ cup onions, chopped into 1 inch pieces
½ cup spring onions
½ cup tofu

RED GARLIC SAUCE
½ cup vegetable broth
3 tbsp tamari soya sauce
(gluten-free soy sauce)
1 tbsp teriyaki coconut aminos
½ tsp sesame oil
2 tbsp chinese rice wine vinegar
l tsp sriracha sauce
½ tsp chilli paste
1 tsp cornstarch
2 tbsp peanut oil
2 tsp garlic, finely chopped
1 ½ tsp ginger, finely chopped
2 tomatoes

1   In a large pot, bring 3-4 cups of water and the avocado oil to boil, cook the noodles for 2-3 minutes. This will be less than the directions on the packaging.

2   Drain and rinse the noodles with cool water. Spread the noodles on a clean kitchen towel to cool fully.

3   In a non-stick pan, heat 1 ½ tbsp of oil over medium high heat. Add the boiled noodles, flattening them on the bottom of the pan to create a flat pancake. Cook uncovered for 6-7 minutes, or until crisp. Flip the noodle pancake and repeat the same process on the other side. Remove the pan from heat.

4   In a medium bowl, mix all of the ingredients for the sauce except for the garlic, ginger and tomato. Whisk and set aside.

5   Boil the tomato in a pan with hot water until the skin begins to pull away. Cool the tomatoes and blend.

6   Over medium high heat, saute the garlic and ginger for 1-2 minutes. Add the blended tomato and cook for another 4-5 minutes. Add the sauce mixture and mix until combined, bring the mixture to a boil then reduce heat and simmer for a few minutes until it thickens.

7   In a large wok, heat oil over high heat. Add the beans and the brussel sprout and cook for 1-2 minutes. Add the bamboo shoots and cook for another minute. Add the bell pepper and onions, cook for one more minute or until the veggies are cooked through. The vegetables are put in the wok depending upon the time needed to cook each of them.

8   Add the tofu and stir fry for 2-3 minutes. Add the cut spring onions and remove the wok from heat.

9   Pour the sauce, tofu & vegetables over crispy noodles and serve .

INDIAN

Curd Rice

Prep time: 5 mins • Cook time: 30 mins
Serves: 2-3

1   When cooking your rice, double the amount of suggested water. After cooking, strain the rice. Move to a bowl, cover and allow to cool in the fridge overnight.

2   In a large bowl, add the non-dairy yogurt and whisk well. If thick, then pour enough water to thin the yogurt so that it can coat the rice fully. Stir in cream of tartar and salt. Add the coconut and the carrots.

3   Add the rice to the yogurt mix and set aside.

4   In a small saucepan heat up the oil of your choice (coconut is suggested for added flavor). Add the mustard seeds. When the seeds begin to splutter add curry leaves, cashews, split chickpea, split black gram, chillies and ginger and roast on medium high until the lentils & the cashews are golden.

5   Add this sautéd lentils & curry leaves mix to the rice & yogurt mixture and mix until combined. Allow to chill in the fridge for another 20-25 minutes before serving.

AUTHORS TIP
•   Instead of rice you can also use cauliflower rice to get a low carbohydrate dish.

½ cup white rice
1 cup non-dairy yogurt
2 tbsp fresh coconut, grated
1 ½ tbsp carrots, shredded
1 ½ tsp black mustard seeds
2 green chili, chopped into big chunks
1 tsp ginger, finely chopped
8-10 curry leaves
5-6 cashews, broken
1 tsp split chickpea lentil
1 tsp split black gram lentil
1 ½ tbsp coconut oil or avocado oil
½ tsp cream of tartar
Salt to taste

Butter Chicken

Prep time: 15 mins • Cook time: 30 mins • Serves: 4-5

1 ½ lb boneless chicken thighs
1 ½ tbsp chicken tandoori masala
1 tbsp olive oil
7-8 large roma tomatoes
3 tbsp coconut oil (butter flavor)
½ tsp shahi jeera (black cumin seeds)
4 tbsp cashews (soaked overnight)
½ tsp red chilli powder
2 tsp kasoori methi (dried fenugreek leaves)
½ tsp garam masala
¼ monk sugar sweetener
½ cup almond milk or oat milk
¼ cup water
Salt to taste

1   In a medium bowl combine the chicken, olive oil and tandoori masala. Marinate for 4 hours.

2   Puree the tomatoes in a blender until smooth.

3   In a medium pan, heat oil over medium heat. Add the black cumin and stir for 30 seconds, until fragrant. Add the pureed tomatoes and cook until the juice of the tomato evaporates and the oil separates.

4   Combine the cashews with water and blend until it has become a thick, smooth paste. Add the cashew paste, red chili powder, garam masala and salt to the tomato puree. Sauté for 1-2 minutes. Reduce the heat to low, slowly add in the milk. Stir until combined.

5   In an air fryer preheated to 400°F cook the chicken for 15 minutes, or until slightly brown. Flip the chicken halfway through after about 8 minutes of cooking. Add the chicken to the tomato curry and simmer for 3-4 minutes. Bring to a boil, then immediately reduce the heat to low.

6   Add the dried fenugreek leaves and simmer for another 3-5 minutes. Serve with gluten-free roti or naan.

AUTHORS TIP
•   If you do not have an airfryer, bake the chicken at 375°F for 25 minutes, then broil at 450°F for another 2-3 minutes.

Cocktail Idlis

Prep time: 5 mins
Cook time: 25 mins
Serves: 4-5

3 cups white rice
1 cup urad dal/white split dal
1 tsp fenugreek seeds
1 ½ tsp mustard seeds
½ tsp idli chutney powder or idli podi
½ tsp amchur or dry mango powder
Pinch of pure asafoetida
(make sure it's gluten-free!)
¼ tsp red chilli powder
2 tbsp coconut oil
15-17 curry leaves
Salt to taste

1   In two separate bowls, soak the white rice and urad dal overnight.

2   After soaking, rinse the rice and grind in small batches until it forms a paste. The rice should not be thick, but should be smooth. Grind the dal and the fenugreek seeds into a paste.

3   Mix the ground pastes, cover and leave in a warm place to ferment overnight. The mixture should begin to rise.

4   In a large pot, boil one cup of water. Lightly coat the wet idli mold with oil, fill with the idli mixture and place in the boiling water. Cover with a lid and allow to steam for approximately 15 minutes. Remove the pot from heat and allow the idlis to cool before removing from the mold.

5   In a medium pan heat the coconut oil over medium high heat. When the oil is hot, add pure asafoetida (gluten-free), mustard seeds and curry leaves. Allow the seeds to splutter. Add idli chutney powder, dry mango powder and red chili powder.

6   Add the cooked idlis and toss with the seasoning until fully coated. Serve warm.

AUTHORS TIP
•   These idlis are also delicious with a coconut chutney!

Punjabi Rajma

Prep time: 5 mins • Cook time: 45 mins • Serves: 2

1 ¼ cup red kidney beans
1 large red onion, chopped
7-8 garlic pods
I inch long piece of ginger
3-4 green chillies
4 large tomatoes, cut into big chunks
2 tbsp avocado oil
1 tsp sugar Salt to taste Cilantro for garnish

1 Soak the kidney beans for at least 3-4 hrs.

2 Add the kidney beans, onions and salt to the Instapot. Add at least 3 cups of water and pressure cook on high for 35 minutes. Quick release the pressure.

3 Grind the garlic, ginger and chilies in a food processor until a thick paste is formed. Remove the paste.

4 Puree the tomatoes in the blender separately.

5 Heat the avocado oil in a deep pot on the stove. Add the garlic/ginger paste and sauté for 3-4 minutes. Add the tomato puree and sauté until the tomatoes have separated from the oil.

6 Add the cooked tomato mix to the kidney beans in the Instapot. Add the sugar and mix until combined. Place the lid on the Instapot and set on sauté mode for 7-8 minutes stirring occasionally in between.

7 Garnish with cilantro and serve over rice.

Potato Corn

Prep time: 5 mins
Cook time: 12 mins
Serves: 2-3

1 ½ cup frozen corn
1 small potato, diced
2 small green chilis
Tajin Mexican seasoning
2 tbsp vegan butter

1 Boil the cubed potatoes until fork tender.

2 Microwave the frozen corn until defrosted, or if using fresh corn boil it separately.

3 In a medium pan, heat olive oil and vegan butter. When the butter is melted, add the finely chopped chilies and potatoes. Sauté until the potatoes reach a golden brown color. Add the corn. If necessary, add more butter to the mixture.

4 Season with butter and Tajin to taste. Serve immediately.

AUTHORS TIP
• This dish can be eaten both warm and cold.

Vegetable Quinoa Pilaf
with Palak Raita

Prep time: 10 mins • Cook time: 15-17 mins
Serves: 4

PILAF
1 cup quinoa
1 cup red onion, chopped
1 cup corn, defrosted
1 cup carrot, chopped
½ cup frozen peas
1 small potato, cubed small
1 tbsp ginger & garlic paste
½ tbsp cumin seeds
¼ tsp turmeric powder
1 tbsp chili powder
1 bay leaf
½ tsp cumin powder
1 tsp coriander powder
¾ tsp lemon rice powder
(gluten-free)
3 tbsp coconut oil - butter flavour
Cilantro to garnish

RAITA
1 cup cashew yogurt
(or alternative dairy-free yogurt)
½ tsp cumin powder
½ red onion, diced small
½ cup spinach, chopped
1 tsp cumin seeds
½ tsp of green chilli, deseeded &
chopped
Salt to taste

FOR THE PILAF

1 Set the Instapot to sauté mode and add oil, cumin seeds, bay leaf and ginger garlic paste. Allow to sauté for approximately 30 seconds before adding the onions. Cook until translucent. Add the corn, carrots, peas and potatoes. Stir fry the vegetables for 3-4 minutes. Add the turmeric, chili powder, cumin powder, coriander powder and lemon rice powder. Sauté for another 2-3 minutes.

2 Rinse the quinoa thoroughly and add to the sautéed vegetables. Stir until just combined. Add 1 cup lukewarm water, secure the Instapot lid and set to rice mode.

3 When cooked through, garnish with cilantro and serve with palak raita.

FOR THE RAITA

1 Heat 1 tsp of oil over medium heat. Add the cumin seeds and onions. Sauté the onions until slightly crispy, then add the spinach. Cook until the spinach begins to shrivel. Remove from heat and cool completely.

2 Mix the yogurt, cumin powder, chili and salt until fully combined. Mix in the spinach and onion. Garnish with cilantro and refrigerate until cold. Serve with the pilaf.

Egg Curry

Prep time: 10 mins • Cook time: 40 mins • Serves: 6

6 eggs, boiled
2-4 tbsp coconut oil
2 ½ small red onions,
finely chopped
12-14 curry leaves
4-5 small tomatoes, pureed
1 tsp fennel seeds
1 tsp mustard seeds
5-6 tbsp distilled vinegar
7-8 dry red chillies
¾ tsp turmeric powder
1 tbsp coriander powder
2 ½ cups coconut milk
⅔ cup lady's fingers, sliced lengthwise

1 Soak the red chillies in vinegar for at least one hour. Grind the soaked red chilies to a paste.

2 In a pan over medium high, heat the coconut oil. Add the mustard seeds, fennel and curry leaves. As soon as the oil begins to pop, add the onions. Saute until the onions are golden brown.

3 Add the ground chili paste to the onions. Sauté for 2 more minutes.

4 Add the coriander and turmeric and stir. Add the tomato puree and salt. Sauté until the tomatoes dry and the water has mostly evaporated. Add the coconut milk and boil for an additional 3-4 minutes.

5 Slice the boiled eggs lengthwise. Lightly spray the lady's fingers with oil and cook in the air fryer for 7-8 minutes.

6 Add the eggs and the cooked lady's fingers to the curry and serve with rice or quinoa.

AUTHORS TIP
• If you would like prawns or fish curry, simply cook the raw prawns or white fish in the coconut milk instead of adding the eggs and lady's fingers.

Oats Lentil Pakora

with Tomato Relish

Prep time: 5 mins
Cook time: 20 mins
Serves: 2-3

OATS PAKORA
¾ cup steel-cut oats
¼ cup bengal gram split
(yellow lentil)
2-3 dry red chillies
¼ cup spinach, chopped
A pinch of cumin powder
A pinch of dry mango powder
1 red onion, chopped
1 green chilli, chopped
1 tablespoon chopped cilantro
½ cup almond milk or oat milk
Olive oil or avocado oil for frying Salt

TOMATO RELISH
2-3 ripe tomatoes, cut into chunks
2 tsp split chickpea lentils
2 tsp split black gram lentils
2 tsp raw peanuts
4 full dry red chillies
¼ tsp jaggery powder
¼ tsp turmeric powder
8-10 curry leaves
1 tbsp distilled vinegar
1 ½ tsp coconut oil
Salt

OATS PAKORA

1   In hot water, soak the yellow lentil with the red chillies for 40 minutes then strain and grind in a food processor. Pour the paste into a large bowl.

2   Grind the steel-cut oats and add to the paste. Then add onions, spinach, salt, cumin powder, dry mango powder, cilantro and non-dairy milk. Mix until fully combined and a thick, but smooth, paste has formed. If it is too thick, add another tablespoon of non-dairy milk. If it is too runny, add another tablespoon of ground steel-cut oats.

3   Heat a large pot with approximately one inch of oil for frying. Divide the oat mixture into 8 equal parts. Shape the mixture into small balls. If the mixture is sticking, wet your hands to shape. Fry the oat balls on medium high until golden brown. Serve with the tomato relish.

TOMATO RELISH

1   Heat oil in a pan on medium high. Add red chilis, lentils and peanuts. For less spice, reduce the amount of chili used.

2   Reduce heat to low and roast the mixture until the peanuts are golden brown. Add curry leaves, and allow to settle before adding tomatoes, turmeric and salt. Sauté till the tomatoes are mushy.

3   Add vinegar and jaggery powder to the pan and saute for another 3-4 minutes then remove the pan from the heat.

4   Allow the mixture to cool, then blend in the food processor until a thick paste is formed. Serve this tangy tomato paste with hot lentil pakoras.

Spicy Shirataki Rice

Prep time: 10 mins
Cook time: 20 mins
Serves: 2

2 packets shirataki rice
2 small sweet potatoes, boiled & cubed
½ cup sweet peas,
shelled & boiled
1 onion, finely chopped
2 tbsp coconut oil or avocado oil
7-8 curry leaves
1½ tsp mustard seeds
½ tsp cream of tartar
½ tsp turmeric
½ tsp garam masala
Salt to taste

1 In a large pan, heat the oil. Add the curry leaves and mustard seeds. When the seeds begin to pop, add the onions and saute until golden brown. Add the sweet potato and sauté for another 3-4 minutes.

2 Boil the shirataki rice in salted water for 5-7 minutes and strain.

3 Add the cooked rice and boiled peas to the pan with the onions and sweet potatoes.

4 Add turmeric, garam masala and cream of tartar mixing until the potatoes are coated. Cook for 5-7 minutes, until the spices are combined and the rice and vegetables are fully coated.

5 Garnish with cilantro and serve immediately.

Cardamom Goat Meat Stew

Prep time: 15 mins • Cook time: 1 hour • Serves: 3-4

1 ½ lbs goat meat chops
1 ½ lbs tomatoes,diced
20-25 green cardamom
3-4 cloves
1 teaspoon red chilli powder
1 teaspoon turmeric
1 ½ tbsp avocado oil
1 black cardamom
Salt to taste
Cilantro

1 Switch on the Instapot on sauté mode. Add avocado oil and cloves. Sauté until aromatic and slightly browned.

2 Add the tomatoes and sauté for 18-20 minutes or until the tomatoes become soft and mushy. Add salt.

3 Add the goat meat to the pot and sauté for another 7-10 minutes until the meat is browned. Add turmeric and red chili powder, black cardamom and sauté for another 3-4 minutes.

4 Grind the green cardamom roughly. Add 3-4 cups of hot water and ground cardamom. Close the lid and the steam valve.

5 Cook the meat on high pressure for 20-25 minutes. Allow the pressure to be released naturally.

6 Garnish with cilantro and serve over rice or as a soup.

AUTHORS TIP
• A pressure cooker can be used over the stove instead of an Instapot.

Chickpea & Potato Curry

Prep time: 10 mins • Cook time: 25 mins
Serves: 4

¾ cup chickpeas
2 potatoes
2 large tomatoes,
finely chopped
4 tbsp avocado oil
1 brown cardamom
2 cloves
1 bunch coriander
1 tsp baking soda
1 inch piece ginger, finely chopped
¾ tsp cumin seeds
¼ tsp fenugreek seeds
¾ tsp dry mango powder
2 tsp coriander powder
A pinch of gluten-free asafoetida

1 Soak the chickpeas overnight and drain. In a large bowl add the baking soda to the chickpeas and mix thoroughly with your hands until coated. Set aside and let it sit for 30 minutes. Rinse the chickpeas to remove excess baking soda.

2 In a pressure cooker boil 2 cups of water. Add the chickpeas, cloves and cardamom. Secure the pressure cooker lid and cook on high heat. When the whistle starts to sound, reduce the heat to low and cook for 10 more minutes.

3 Strain the chickpeas, keeping the water. Set aside.

4 Boil the potatoes until soft, and cut into ½ inch cubes.

5 Heat the oil in a pan on low and add the cumin and fenugreek seeds. Cook until aromatic and slightly browned, then mix in the asafoetida and ginger.

6 Add the tomatoes. Cook until the tomatoes begin to break down and the oil begins to rise to the top of the pan. Add the remaining dry spices.

7 Add the boiled chickpeas and boiled potatoes. Sauté for 5-7 minutes. Add 1 ½ cup leftover chickpea water and bring to a boil. Thicken the mixture by mashing some of the chickpeas, mix and cook for an additional 2 minutes.

8 Garnish with coriander leaves and serve with a grain of your choosing!

AUTHORS TIP
• Use the canned organic chickpeas can to save time.

ITALIAN

Spinach Mushroom Pizza

Prep time: 25 mins
Cook time : 25 mins Serves: 4

PIZZA DOUGH
3 cups cassava flour
1 cup potato flour
½ cup psyllium water
½ cup lukewarm water
3 heaped tsp dried instant gluten-free yeast
½ tsp honey
½ tsp salt
1 ½ tablespoon vegan butter

PIZZA SAUCE
2 cup cashews (soaked overnight)
½ cup nutritional yeast
2 tsp Dijon mustard
6 cloves garlic
2 tsp cayenne pepper
Salt & pepper to taste
2 tbsp vegan butter

RECOMMENDED PIZZA TOPPINGS
Sauteed spinach
Sauteed onions
Green bell peppers
Mushroom
Onions
Artichoke
Dairy-free mozzarella
Dairy-free ricotta
Zucchini & tomato is another good topping combination

PIZZA DOUGH

1 In a small bowl mix together honey, yeast and lukewarm water. Let this stand until the yeast is dissolved and the mixture is frothy. About 2-3 minutes.

2 In a medium mixing bowl, combine non-dairy milk, vegan butter, salt and yeast mixture.

3 In a separate bowl mix together all of the dry ingredients. Gradually add the wet ingredients to the flour mixture, stirring until just combined. Knead the dough into a smooth ball. Add any additional flour as needed, stirring until the dough forms a cohesive ball, and begins to pull away from the sides of the bowl.

4 Brush the dough ball with melted butter or olive oil and cover loosely with plastic wrap. Leave in a warm area to rise for 4-6 hours till it almost doubles.

5 Remove dough from the plastic wrap and divide into four parts. Roll out into pizza crust and with fork poke holes in the crust and bake at 400°F for approximately 10 minutes. Set aside.

PIZZA SAUCE

1 Blend soaked cashews in a food processor until it becomes a thick paste, about 3-5 minutes, adding water as needed.

2 Mix in the nutritional yeast, mustard, garlic, cayenne pepper and salt & pepper to taste. Sauce should be thick and creamy.

TOPPINGS

1 Drizzle oil into a small pan. Add chopped onions and cook over medium heat for 10-15 minutes until caramelized, stirring occasionally.

2 In a second pan coated with oil saute the spinach until slightly wilted. Remove the spinach from the pan, add more oil if needed and saute the mushrooms until golden. Add approximately 1 tbsp of vegan butter when sauteeing for best results.

ASSEMBLE YOUR PIZZA

1 Coat the pizza dough with a generous layer of the cashew sauce. Layer the spinach and mushroom right on top of the sauce, adding any other desired toppings. Sprinkle the pizza with dairy free mozzarella.

2 Bake at 400°F for about 10-15 minutes until cheese is melted and edges of the dough are golden brown. Dairy free mozzarella takes longer to melt than dairy cheese, so be patient.

3 When the pizza is almost done remove from the oven and spoon dollops of the ricotta cheese and caramelized onions on top of the pizza. Put it back in the oven and bake for 2-3 minutes until the cheese is fully melted and toppings are warm. Slice up the pizza and serve!

AUTHORS TIPS

• This should yield 4 pizza bases and stays fresh for about 15 days when frozen!

• Incase the yeast mixture does not become frothy, then discard it and start again. Chances are that the water was not lukewarm and hence the yeast died so no froth.

Miso Pasta

**Prep time: 5 mins Cook time: 15 mins
Serves: 4**

4 strips low-sodium bacon
2 tbsp chili garlic paste
2 tbsp miso paste
3 eggs
1 box gluten-free spaghetti
½ cup dairy-free parmesan cheese
2 stalks green onions,
chopped

1 Boil your pasta in salted water according to the instructions on the box until al dente. Save approximately a cup of pasta water when draining the noodles. Run the hot pasta noodles under cold water immediately after draining until cooled.

2 Cut your bacon strips into ¾ of an inch pieces and sauté in a hot pan until cooked and crispy. In a bowl, add 2 tablespoons of miso paste, 2 tablespoons of garlic chili paste and 2 tablespoons of warm pasta water. Whisk together until combined. Add eggs and whisk again until combined.

3 Remove excess bacon grease from your pan, leaving desired amount for flavor. Add your cooked pasta to the pan with your bacon. Reduce heat to low and add the miso egg mixture. Stir until combined.

4 Cook on low until heated all the way through and the sauce mixture has thickened to desired consistency. If it begins to become clumpy immediately remove from heat. Garnish with chopped green onions and serve.

Mushroom & Oats Risotto

Prep time: 15 mins • Cook time: 30 mins • Serves: 3

¾ cup portobello mushroom
1 cup porcini mushroom
5-7 garlic cloves, roughly chopped
3 tbsp coconut oil (butter flavor)
3 tsp vegan butter
¾ cup gluten-free steel cut oats
1 large white onion, finely chopped
2 cups chicken broth or vegetable broth
4 tbsp rice wine vinegar
½ cup vegan parmesan cheese
3-4 tbsp parsley finely chopped
1 tsp lemon pepper
Salt to taste

1   Sauté onions in a large pan with 1 ½ tbsp of coconut oil on medium-high heat until golden brown. Add the steel cut oats and saute for another 3-4 minutes.

2   Reduce heat to medium, add the chicken broth and cook until boiling. When most of the broth has been absorbed add 2 tbsp of rice wine vinegar & a dash of salt. Cook until the oats are tender and chewy. If the oats are still firm, add more broth and continue to cook until desired texture is reached.

3   In another large pan, heat the remaining coconut oil and fry the garlic on medium high heat until golden. Add the sliced mushrooms and continue cooking on medium heat until tender. Add the remaining vinegar, lemon pepper and salt to taste.

4   Combine the mushroom mixture with the oat mixture and add parmesan cheese. Mix until the cheese melts. Add parsley, mix well & serve hot.

18 ounces gluten-free fettuccine pasta
1 cup cashews, soaked overnight
1/3 cup nutritional yeast
3-4 cloves garlic
½ cup shiitake mushrooms
½ cup cremini mushrooms
4 tbsp truffle oil
2 tbsp vegan butter
6 sprigs thyme
2 tsp lemon juice
1 tsp garlic powder
2 tsp lemon pepper
Salt to taste

Truffle Mushroom Pasta

Prep time: 10 mins • Cook time: 15 mins • Serves: 3

1 Blend the cashews for 2-3 minutes, or until they become a thick paste. Add nutritional yeast, garlic, and salt to taste. Blend until combined. If the paste is too thick, add water to reach desired consistency. Set mixture aside.

2 Cook pasta according to package instructions. Strain and set aside, adding a few drops of truffle oil so that the pasta do not stick together.

3 In a large frying pan sauté shiitake and crimini mushrooms in vegan butter over medium heat until caramelized, about 5-7 minutes. Add lemon pepper, garlic powder, lemon juice and salt to taste. Stir until mushrooms are coated.

4 Add blended cashew paste and remaining truffle oil to the mushrooms. Cook for 3-5 minutes on medium heat.

5 Reduce the heat to low, add pasta and thyme and cook for another 5 minutes.

6 Garnish with fresh thyme and serve immediately!

Italian Macaroni Salad

Prep time: 15 mins • Cook time: 30 mins • Serves: 3

½ cup olive oil
¼ cup white wine vinegar
½ cup dairy-free parmesan (optional)
1 tsp dijon mustard
2 garlic cloves
1 tsp oregano
1 tsp chili flakes
8 ounces rotini chickpea pasta
1 cup cherry tomatoes, halved
1 cup cucumbers, diced
½ cup onions, diced
1 cup bell peppers, chopped
¼ cup parsley
10 leaves basil
Italian herbs seasoning
Salad spring mix

1   Cook your pasta according to instructions on the package. Strain pasta and run under cold water until cool.

2   In a food processor add olive oil, white wine vinegar, dairy-free parmesan, dijon mustard, garlic, chili flakes and oregano and blend until creamy.

3   Rinse and chop cucumbers. Combine with tomatoes. Rinse and chop bell peppers, keeping them separate.

4   In a small pan with oil, lightly saute bell peppers until slightly tender. Finely chop parsley and basil.

5   Combine all ingredients except the spring mix into a large bowl and mix. Add the mustard dressing, salt and pepper and mix until everything is well coated.

6   Chill in the fridge for 20 minutes. Right before serving add a heapful of spring salad and mix together!

Green Pasta

Prep time: 10 mins
Cook time: 25 mins
Serves: 3

1 ¼ cup edamame beans
1 cup baby spinach
½ cup mushroom, chopped into small squares
2 spring onions, chopped vertically
4-5 brussel sprouts, thinly sliced
¼ cup marinated artichokes hearts, chopped
1 tbsp tahini
2-3 garlic cloves
2 tbsp nutritional yeast
1 tbsp rice wine vinegar
½ tsp apple cider vinegar
1 tbsp fresh lemon juice
½ tsp onion powder
1 tsp oregano
Garlic salt to taste
3 tbsp olive oil
1 tbsp vegan butter
2 tbsp basil paste
8 ounces chickpea rotini or gluten-free spaghetti
1 tbsp dairy-free parmesan

1 Cook the pasta according to the instructions on the packaging.

2 Blend the edamame, tahini, garlic, rice wine vinegar, apple cider vinegar, lemon juice and onion powder until a smooth paste is formed.

3 In a medium pan, heat 1 tsp olive oil and the vegan butter. Saute the mushrooms for 5-7 minutes. Add the brussel sprouts and saute for another 1-2 minutes. Add the spinach and saute until it wilts.

4 Add the spring onions and artichoke hearts, then remove from heat.

5 In another pan, heat the remaining oil. Add the basil paste and saute for 1 minute. Add the bean paste and saute for another 2-3 minutes, then add the pasta. Cook until the bean paste coats and sticks to the pasta.

6 Fold the cooked vegetables to the pasta, sprinkle with dairy-free parmesan and serve.

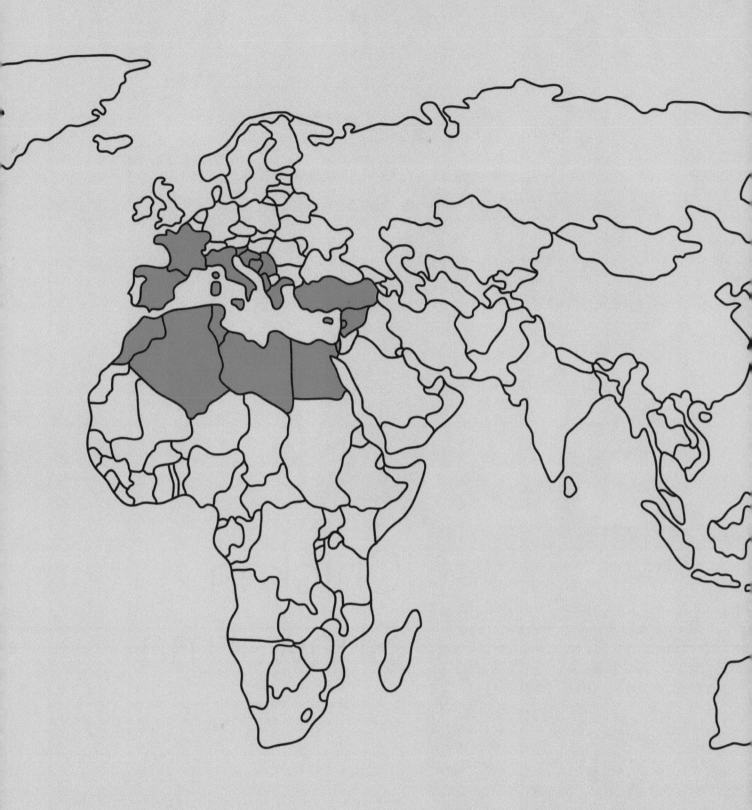

MEDITERRANEAN

Prep time: 10 mins
Cook time: 15 mins
Serves: 4-5

8 boneless skinless chicken thighs
3 tbsp olive oil or avocado oil
2 tbsp lemon juice
½ tsp garlic powder
¾ tsp lemon pepper
1 tsp cayenne pepper
1 tsp cumin powder
2 tsp coriander powder
2 tsp mediterranean spice mix
2 small garlic cloves, finely chopped

Chicken Shawarma

1 Combine all of the ingredients except the chicken in a medium bowl. Transfer to a large zip lock bag and add the chicken. Seal and massage the chicken so that each piece is well coated with the marinade. Allow the chicken and marinade to sit for 6-8 hours.

2 Heat a grill to 375°F and place the chicken on it, leaving space between the pieces. Cook on each side for 3-5 minutes until charred. If you do not have a grill, heat a pan or cast iron over high heat. Cook the chicken on each side for 4-6 minutes, regularly checking that it is not becoming dry.

3 Serve the chicken with fattoush salad, or use it to make shawarma rolls.

Fattoush Salad

Prep time: 20 mins • Cook time: 10 mins • Serves: 6

FOR THE SALAD
2 gluten-free tortillas, cut into chips shape
½ english cucumber,
peeled and diced
½ cup lettuce
2 ½ tbsp parsley, chopped
3-4 spring onions, chopped
2 tbsp mint, chopped
2 tbsp coriander, chopped
7-8 cherry tomatoes, halved
3 round red radish, thinly sliced
Olive oil baking spray

FOR THE DRESSING
½ cup olive oil
4-5 tablespoons lemon juice
3 garlic cloves, crushed
½ tsp sumac
1 tsp lemon pepper
Salt to taste

1   Lightly coat the tortilla chips with olive oil and place in the air fryer. Fry at 375°F for 4-5 minutes, or until golden and crispy. Remove from the air fryer and set aside.

2   In a medium bowl, whisk all of the ingredients for the dressing until combined. Cover and refrigerate until it is time to serve.

3   In a large bowl, combine all of the ingredients for the salad. Cover and refrigerate until it is time to serve.

4   Drizzle the dressing onto the salad just before serving. Toss well and add the chips.

5   Sprinkle the salad with sumac and serve immediately.

1   In a small pan over medium high heat sauté the chopped garlic until th oil begins to bubble. Add the chillies and cook for one minute more. Add the za'atar powder and cream of tartar and cook for 2 minutes. Remove the pan from heat.

2   Add the sumac after removing the pan from heat.

3   Lightly toast the pita over a low flame. Spread a thin layer of cream cheese over the pita. Top one half of the pita with the za'atar mixture and cubed mozzarella.

4   Fold the pita in half to make a semicircle. In a lightly oiled pan fry the pita on both sides over a low flame until browned.

5   Cut into triangles and serve immediately.

Lebanese Bread with Za'atar & Sumac

Prep time: 10 mins • Cook time: 10 mins • Serves: 3

2 gluten-free pita breads or cassava tortilla wraps
1 tbsp garlic, minced
¼ cup fresh dairy-free mozzarella, cubed
1 ½ tbsp red chillies, chopped
3 tbsp dairy-free cream cheese
2 ½ tbsp olive oil or avocado oil
3-4 tsp za'atar
½ tsp cream of tartar
¼ tsp sumac powder

Crispy Chickpeas

Prep time: 10 mins • Cook time: 20 mins
Serves: 4

1 cup chickpeas (soaked overnight)
2 tsp corn flour
1 tsp rice powder
½ tsp red chilli powder
2 tsp dried mint leaves
1 tsp oregano
Olive oil to fry

1 1 In a small pot, boil the soaked chickpeas for 10 minutes until they are soft. Remove the pot from heat and allow them to cool.

2 In a medium bowl, combine the corn flour, salt and chickpeas.

3 In a deep pan, heat about 2 inches of oil and add the chickpeas. Fry the chickpeas on medium heat until crispy. Remove the chickpeas from the oil and set on a plate covered with a paper towel to drain any oil.

4 Sprinkle the chickpeas with red chili powder, mint and oregano. Toss until the chickpeas are coated and serve.

Falafel

Prep time: 45 mins
Cook time: 15 mins
Serves: 3-4

1 cup chickpeas, soaked overnight
½ yellow/white onion, roughly chopped
¼ cup scallions (optional)
¾ cup parsley, chopped
¾ cup cilantro, chopped
2 small seedless chilies
¼ tsp turmeric
¼ tsp garlic salt
2 garlic cloves
1 tsp ground cumin
¼ tsp lemon pepper
2 tbsp chickpea flour
½ tsp baking soda
Olive oil or avocado oil for frying
Salt to taste

1   Drain the soaked chickpeas and blend in a food processor until smooth. Add the onions, parsley, cilantro, green onions, chilies, garlic, garlic salt, turmeric, cumin powder, lemon powder and salt to the food processor. Using the pulse setting, blend the mixture until it becomes a thick paste.

2   Transfer the paste into a bowl. With a rubber spatula, fold in the chickpea flour and baking soda. If the mixture is too thick, add water 1 tablespoon at a time until it thins. If the mixture is too thin, add chickpea flour 1 teaspoon at a time until it becomes thick enough.

3   Using a spoon or ice cream scoop, make 1 inch balls and transfer to a lined baking sheet.

4   In a deep pan, heat at least 3 inches of oil. Fry the falafel balls over medium high heat until browned on the outside and cooked through. Remove the falafel from the oil and set on a paper towel to drain. Serve immediately!

Tabbouleh with Chicken

Prep time: 40 mins • Cook time: 10 mins
Makes 4 pancakes

½ cup quinoa
8 ounces chicken, diced
½ red onion, diced
2 tbsp olive oil
½ tsp cumin powder
½ tsp lemon pepper
½ tsp cinnamon powder
¼ cup pine nuts
½ cup parsley, finely chopped
¼ cup mint finely, chopped
¼ cup cilantro, finely chopped
½ cup roma tomatoes, diced
½ cup cucumber, diced
Salt to taste

1   In a medium pot, bring 1 cup water, quinoa and salt to a boil. Reduce the heat to low, cover and allow it to simmer for another 5 minutes.

2   Remove the pot from heat and allow the quinoa to steam for 5 more minutes. Using a fork, fluff the quinoa.

3   In a lightly oiled medium pan sauté the onions until translucent. Add the chicken and sauté for 6-7 minutes over medium heat, or until the chicken turns golden.

4   Add the cumin powder, salt, lemon pepper and cinnamon and fry for 2-3 minutes, stirring occasionally. Add the pine nuts and cook until lightly roasted. Remove from heat and set aside to cook.

5   In a mason jar, add all of the ingredients for the dressing and shake well until fully combined.

6   In a large bowl, combine the parsley, mint, cilantro, cucumber, and tomatoes. Mix well. Add the quinoa, chicken and dressing. Toss and serve cold.

AMERICAN

Mushroom & Spinach Stuffed Buckwheat Pancakes

Prep time: 25 mins
Cook time: 30 mins • Serves: 12

FOR THE BATTER
1 cup buckwheat flour
¼ tsp baking powder
1 cup dairy-free cashew yogurt, unsweetened
1 ½ tbsp apple cider vinegar
½ tsp cream of tartar
¼ - ½ cup of water
1 tsp ginger paste
3 green chilli, finely chopped
¼ cup cilantro, finely chopped
Salt to taste

FOR THE FILLING
3 tbsp avocado oil
1 tsp garlic, chopped
1 small white onion, chopped
1 cup mushroom, thinly sliced
3 cups spinach, chopped
½ cup shelled sweet corn
8 ounces skinless, boneless chicken, chopped small (optional)
½ tsp cumin powder
½ tsp red chilli powder
½ tsp lemon pepper
½ tsp cream of tartar
2 tsp tabasco
Dairy-free fresh mozzarella cheese, cubed

FOR THE BATTER
1 In a blender mix the yogurt, apple cider vinegar, water and cream of tartar. Blend until smooth.

2 In a separate bowl mix the buckwheat flour, ginger paste, coriander, salt, baking powder, and chilis. Add the yogurt mixture and mix well until it becomes a smooth batter. Let the batter rest for an hour.

FOR THE FILLING
1 Heat the oil in the pan . Add the chicken and sauté for 7-8 minutes until it begins to turn golden brown.

2 Heat 1 ½ tablespoons of oil in another pan. Add the garlic and sauté until golden brown. Add the onions and sauté until translucent. Add the mushroom and sauté on medium high heat for another 7 minutes, or until cooked.

3 Add the cumin powder and chili powder. Mix fully, Add the chicken into the mushroom mixture. Add the spinach and boiled sweet corn. Sauté for 2 minutes then add the cream of tartar, tabasco and salt. Turn off the heat and add the cubed mozzarella. Mix until combined.

4 Grease a non-stick pan with cooking oil. Pour an even layer of batter into the pan and cook on medium high until golden brown. Flip the pancake and cook the other side.

5 Spoon desired stuffing onto the pancake and fold, making a semi-circle, and serve.

Prep time: 10 mins
Cook time: 7 mins
Serves: 4

4 cups arugula leaves, washed
3 tbsp extra virgin olive oil
3 tbsp lemon juice
1 tsp dijon mustard
2 garlic cloves
½ tsp lemon pepper
2-3 marinated artichoke hearts
Dairy-free parmesan cheese or Dairy-free parmesan wedge
Salt to taste

Arugula Salad with Artichoke Hearts

1 Place the arugula in a salad bowl. Set aside.

2 Blend the olive oil, lemon juice, mustard, lemon pepper, garlic and salt until fully combined. Pour over the arugula and toss until coated.

3 Use a vegetable peeler to shave the parmesan, and sprinkle over the salad.

4 Separate the artichoke heart petals and add to the salad.

5 Serve immediately.

AUTHORS TIP
• Shredded dairy-free parmesan cheese incase a cheese wedge is not available.

Crispy Popcorn Chicken

Prep time: 15 mins • Cook time: 10 mins • Serves: 2-3

2 large eggs
2 chicken breasts
¾ cup arrowroot flour
¼ cup of rice flour
3 tsp chilli powder
2 tsp onion powder
2 tsp garlic powder
1 tbsp chilli flakes
Pickle juice
Oil for frying

1 Pound the chicken with a wooden or metal mallet to soften. Chop the chicken into one inch pieces and move to a large bowl. Add pickle juice until the chicken is fully submerged, allow to soak for 15 minutes - 3 hours.

2 In a medium sized bowl, beat the eggs until the yolk and whites are fully combined. Drain the pickle juice from the chicken. Coat the chicken with the beaten eggs.

3 In a separate bowl, mix the flour, chili powder, chili flakes, onion powder and garlic powder. Add salt and pepper to taste.

4 Remove the chicken from the egg mixture one piece at a time and dip in the flour mixture to coat fully. Dip it again into the egg mixture, and then in the flour mixture once again. Set aside and repeat until all of the chicken is coated.

5 Fill a medium pot halfway with olive oil or avocado oil. Add the chicken and fry over medium heat for 3 minutes. Flip the chicken and increase the heat to high. Cook the chicken for 1 minute more till crisp and tender.

6 Serve with dairy-free ranch or other desired sauce!

Buffalo Chicken Wings

Prep time: 10 mins
Cook time: 25-30 mins • Serves: 3

1.5 lbs chicken wings
½ tbsp olive oil
¼ tsp lemon pepper
1 tbsp baking powder
½ tsp garlic powder
3 tbsp gluten-free and dairy-free buffalo sauce
1 ½ tbsp dairy-free butter

1 Rinse and pat the chicken wings dry with a paper towel. Toss the wings in oil until coated. Mix the lemon pepper, baking powder and garlic powder and toss with the chicken until each piece is coated.

2 Preheat the air fryer to 390 degrees. Arrange the wings in a single layer in the basket and fry for 10 minutes. Flip the wings and fry for another 10 minutes, or until the fat has begun to drain off the chicken and the skin is becoming crispy.

3 In a large pan, heat the butter and add the buffalo sauce. Add the chicken wings and toss until the chicken is fully coated and begins to dry. Serve with gluten-free and dairy-free ranch and celery sticks.

Lemon Pepper Cauliflower

1 In a large skillet, heat the oil over medium high heat. Add the cauliflower. Sauté for 5 minutes or until golden brown, tossing occasionally. Sprinkle the cauliflower with the lemon pepper and cream of tartar. Remove from heat.

2 Preheat the oven to 450°F.

3 Mix the cornflour and baking powder. Sprinkle the mixture over the cauliflower. Return to the skillet and bake for 10 minutes, or until crisp. Serve immediately.

Prep time: 10 mins • Cook time: 20 mins
Serves: 4

1 large cauliflower, chopped into bite size pieces
2 tsp avocado oil
1 tsp lemon pepper
½ tsp cream of tartar
1 ½ tbsp cornflour
¼ tsp baking powder

Spinach and Pepper Egg Muffins

Prep time: 15 mins
Cook time: 30 mins
Serves: 6

8 organic eggs
2 slices of gluten-free bread
¼ cup dairy-free milk
½ cup bacon
½ cup sweet potato, shredded
¼ cup bell pepper, cubed
½ cup baby spinach, chopped
1 tbsp dairy-free cheddar cheese
Olive oil spray

1   In a medium bowl, mix the shredded sweet potato with olive oil and salt until coated.

2   Cook the bacon in the air fryer for 8-10 minutes.

3   Heat a pan and drizzle with olive oil. Sauté the bell pepper for 1-2 minutes, then add the spinach. Cook until the spinach begins to wilt. Remove from heat and set aside.

4   Grind the bread in a blender.

5   In a small bowl, whisk the eggs, milk, salt, ground bread and cheese.

6   Preheat the oven to 375°F. Spray a muffin tray with olive oil and evenly divide the sweet potato mixture into the muffin cups. Bake for 15 minutes.

7   Remove the tray from the oven. Evenly distribute the bell pepper and spinach mixture into the muffin tray cups. Fill each muffin tray cup with the egg mixture until almost full. Break the bacon into small bits and sprinkle over the eggs. Bake for 8-10 minutes. The eggs should be puffed and firm through the center. Remove the muffin tin carefully using a rubber spatula and serve immediately.

Tangy & Spicy Sweet Potato Focaccia Burger

1 sweet potato
1 can black beans, rinsed
& drained
2 spring onions, chopped
½ white onion, chopped
1 stick celery, chopped
1 small red bell pepper, chopped
1 small capsicum, chopped
2 green chillies, chopped
1 tbsp cream of tartar
¼ tsp dried mango powder
¾ tsp cumin powder
¼ tsp lemon pepper
½ tsp red chilli powder
½ tsp onion powder
½ cup rolled oats, coarsely ground
6 pieces of gluten-free &
dairy-free focaccia bread
1 tomato, sliced
1 avocado, sliced
1 cup alfalfa sprouts

FOR THE SPREAD
2 tbsp mayonnaise
1 tsp sriracha hot sauce
¼ cup lettuce, finely shredded

Prep time: 15 mins • Cook time: 25 mins • Serves: 8

1 Slice the sweet potato in half. Preheat the air fryer to 385°F and cook the halved sweet potato for 10 minutes.

2 Skin the sweet potato. Add to a medium bowl with the black beans and mash until fully combined.

3 Add the chopped vegetable and chili mixture. Add the dry spices and salt, then mix in the rolled oats.

4 Divide into 8 portions and shape into patties.

5 In a skillet heated over medium high, drizzle and heat olive oil. Place the patties one at a time in the pan and cook each side for 4-5 minutes, or until golden brown.

6 In a small bowl, mix the mayonnaise, sriracha and finely shredded lettuce.

7 Heat the focaccia until crisp, and spread the mayonnaise dressing over the bread. Layer the sliced tomatoes, sweet potato patty, and avocado. Top with alfalfa sprouts and serve immediately

Eggs Benedict & Breakfast Potatoes

Prep time: 15 mins Cook time: 40 mins
Serves: 2

HOLLANDAISE SAUCE
4 egg yolks
4 tbsp vegan butter, melted
1-2 tbsp lemon
½ tsp lemon pepper
Salt to taste

POACHED EGG
4 eggs
2 tbsp distilled vinegar
Salt to taste

BREAKFAST POTATOES
2-3 golden potatoes, boiled
Tajin seasoning
¼ tsp garlic powder
¼ tsp cayenne pepper
Salt to taste

EXTRAS
2 gluten & dairy-free English
muffins
4 slices Canadian bacon
1 tbsp chives, finely chopped

AUTHORS TIP
•   If you do not have a double boiler,
heat a few cups of water in a deep
saucepan and place the bowl inside it
to create one.

HOLLANDAISE SAUCE

1   Separate the egg yolks from the egg whites. Whisk the eggs yolks until they become light and fluffy. The eggs should appear to double in size. Add the melted vegan butter slowly, continuously whisking the eggs to avoid curdling.

2   Add the lemon, lemon pepper and a pinch of salt. Whisk until combined.

3   In a double boiler heat a few cups of water. Continue whisking the sauce in the double broiler until it begins to thicken. Remove from heat and continue whisking the mixture until it cools completely.

BREAKFAST POTATOES

1   Dice the boiled potatoes into ½ inch pieces.

2   In a large pan over high heat drizzle oil and add the potatoes in a single layer so that they are laying flat in the pan. Cook for 3-5 minutes without stirring until they become golden. Flip and cook the other side. Add the garlic powder, cayenne pepper, and salt to taste. Mix the potatoes until they are fully coated. Add 3-4 tbsp of water to the pan and cook covered.

3   When the water has cooked off, remove the lid and let the potatoes fry until they are golden brown and crispy. Sprinkle with tajin to taste.

POACHED EGG

1   Fill a large pot halfway with water and bring to a rolling boil. Reduce the heat to medium and add the distilled vinegar.

2   Crack an egg into a small bowl or ladle. Using a large spoon, swirl the water in the pot until a dip is created in the middle of the water. Gently lower the egg into the dip, allowing it to sit for 3-4 minutes in the hot water until firm. Remove the poached egg from the water.

3   Toast a buttered English muffin in a pan lightly coated with oil. Remove from the pan and lay on a plate. Add the Canadian bacon, poached egg and hollandaise sauce on top of the toast. Garnish with chives and serve with the potatoes.

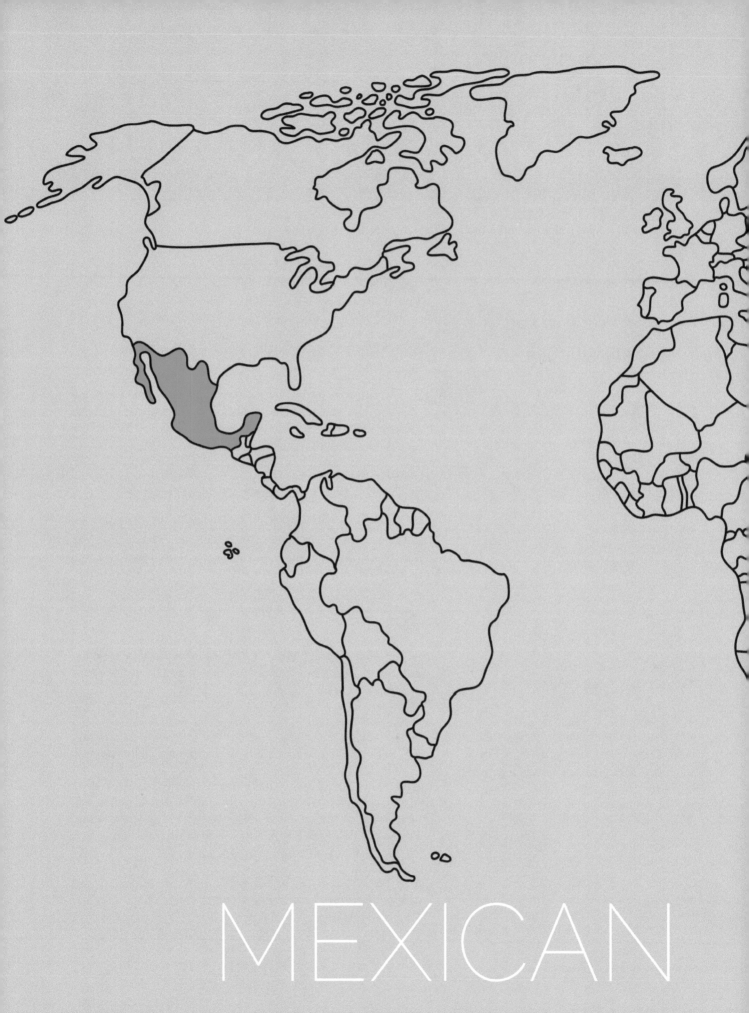

MEXICAN

Corn Fritters

Prep time: 15 mins
Cook time: 15 mins
Serves: 5

½ cup corn starch
¼ cup tapioca flour
¼ cup rice flour
1 tsp baking powder
¾ tsp - 1 tsp tajin
1 tbsp lemon juice
1 tbsp apple cider vinegar
1 tbsp coriander seeds, freshly ground
2 large eggs
1/3 cup almond or oat milk
3 cups fresh cut corn kernels
½ cup green capsicum, diced
¼ cup white onion,
finely chopped
¼ cup carrots, shredded
1-2 tablespoon jalapeno,
finely chopped
¾ cup dairy-free cheese, shredded
Coconut butter

1   Combine the flour, baking powder and seasoning.

2   In a separate bowl, whisk the egg, lemon juice, apple cider vinegar, and dairy-free milk. Add in the dry ingredients and beat well until fully combined, with no clumps.

3   Add the vegetables and cheese. Mix until combined. The batter should be relatively thick, if it is too runny add more flour.

4   Heat a skillet and add approximately 1 tbsp of butter. Over medium heat, place a rounded 2½ inch spoonful of batter in the skillet, flattening with the hand or backside of the spoon. Cook each side until golden brown and crisp.

1 cup rice
7-8 fresh asparagus or green beans, cut into diagonal pieces
1 carrot, shredded
1 green capsicum, finely chopped
1 orange or red bell pepper, finely chopped
1 onion, finely chopped
1 ½ tomato, finely chopped
1 ½ tomato, pureed
2 tsp gluten-free Mexican chilli sauce
6-7 garlic flakes
2-3 whole red chilis
1 tbsp avocado oil
1 tbsp dairy free butter
1 tsp cumin powder
2 sticks cinnamon
3-4 cloves
3-4 black pepper

Spanish Rice

Prep time: 15 mins • Cook time: 25 mins • Serves: 6

1   Rinse the rice to remove the starch. Boil until tender. Sieve and set aside.

2   Steam the beans and set aside. Lightly steam the carrots.

3   Grind the cinnamon, cloves and black pepper until powdered.

4   Using a mortar and pestle, crush the garlic and red chili together.

5   Over medium heat, sauté the onions in butter and oil. Cook until they begin turning brown. Add the garlic chili paste and cook for an additional 2-3 minutes.

6   Add the tomatoes and tomato puree, chili sauce and all of the spices. Cook for 1-2 minutes. Add the carrots, capsicum, steamed beans and rice. Add the salt and toss lightly until combined.

7   Stir fry for 2-3 minutes and serve.

Vegan Nacho Cheese Dip

Prep time: mins • Cook time: mins • Serves:

1 cup golden potatoes, cubed
1 small carrot, chopped
½ cup raw cashews
½ cup unsweetened dairy-free milk
3 tsp olive oil or avocado oil
1 tomato
2 tsp lemon juice
½ tsp lemon pepper
½ tsp garlic powder
½ tsp onion powder
½ tsp cayenne
½ cup nutritional yeast
Salt to taste

1 Soak the cashews overnight.

2 Place the carrots and potatoes in a pan of water and boil until the vegetables become soft.

3 Drain the vegetables and the cashews and combine in a blender. Add the remaining ingredients and blend well.

4 If your dip is too thick, add more milk to thin it out.

Breakfast Burrito

Prep time: 15 mins
Cook time: 30 mins
Serves: 4

8 slices thick cut bacon
3-4 sweet potatoes, boiled and cubed
½ onion, finely chopped
1 red bell pepper, finely chopped
½ - ¾ tsp tajin powder
¼ tsp cayenne pepper
½ tsp cumin powder
7-8 eggs
4-5 tbsp dairy-free milk
1 tbsp butter
2 cups spring greens
5-7 pickled banana pepper, chopped
2 tbsp pickle juice
1 ripe avocado, sliced
3-4 tbsp dairy-free cheddar
cheese
Hot sauce
½ tsp avocado oil

AUTHORS TIP
• Never add the butter directly to a heated skillet as it will burn the butter, always brush with oil first!

1 Preheat an airfryer to 395°F. Spray the sweet potatoes with olive oil and cook in the air fryer for 5-7 minutes, or until crisp.

2 In a lightly greased pan, sauté the onions over medium high heat until translucent. Add the bell pepper and sauté for an additional 5-6 minutes. Add the tajin, cumin, and cayenne pepper and mix until combined.

3 Add the sweet potatoes, toss and set aside.

4 Whisk the eggs and milk until combined. Brush a skillet with oil and heat over a high heat. Add the butter and heat until melted. Add the egg mixture and reduce the heat to medium. Sprinkle the cheese, salt and pepper on the eggs. Allow the eggs to begin cooking, then scramble until just set.

5 In a separate bowl, mix the spring greens, banana peppers and pickle juice and toss.

6 Heat the air fryer to 400°F and cook the bacon for 8 minutes. After 4 minutes, check the bacon and flip if necessary. Cook to desired texture. Remove the bacon from the air fryer and drain on a plate covered in paper towel. Chop the bacon.

TO ASSEMBLE THE BURRITO
1 Heat the tortilla in a flat pan over low heat. Transfer to a plate covered in aluminum foil. Add the spring greens and top with the egg, bacon, avocado and sweet potato. Drizzle with hot sauce.

2 Fold the left and right sides of the tortilla over the filling. Fold the bottom flap of the tortilla over the filling, tucking the sides as you roll. Wrap the foil around the burrito.

3 In the aluminum foil, grill the burrito for 3-4 minutes before serving.

Fish Ceviche

Prep time: 45 mins • Serves: 6

½ red onion, thinly slices
18 ounces fresh sea bass or red snapper
2-3 garlic cloves, minced
¼ tsp black pepper
1 fresh jalapeno chilli, deseeded and chopped
1 cup english cucumber, diced
12-14 cherry tomatoes, diced
1 avocado, chopped
1 cup fresh lime juice, divided
½ cup fresh orange juice, divided
½ cup cilàntro, chopped
1 tbsp mint, chopped
Salt to taste

1   Cut the fish filet into ¼ inch cubes and transfer them to a glass bowl.

2   Add the salt, pepper, jalapeno, garlic, ½ cup lime juice and ¼ cup orange juice to the fish. Completely submerge the fish in the juice and marinate for at least 2 hours.

3   Mix the salt and onions and let stand for at least 15 minutes. Rinse the onions with fresh water and pat dry between 2 pieces of paper towels.

4   Drain the fish. Add the remaining lime juice, orange juice, onions, cucumbers, tomatoes, avocado, cilantro and mint. Toss gently.

5   If desired, add more salt and pepper. Refrigerate for 15-20 minutes and serve.

AUTHORS TIP
•   Do not use a metal bowl, it will alter the taste of the fish. Only use glass or ceramic.

Pork Taco Salad in a Tortilla Bowl

FOR THE BOWL
4 gluten-free tortillas
4 tbsp avocado oil

FOR THE FILLING
15 ounces pork carnitas
(recipe on page --)
2 tbsp dairy-free classic blend cheese
1 15 ounce black beans, drained & rinsed
¼ tsp chilli powder
¼ tsp cumin powder
¼ tsp garlic salt
½ tbsp pickled jalapeno, chopped
1 head romaine lettuce, chopped
1 cup frozen corn, thawed
½ tbsp dairy-free butter
½ tbsp tajin salt
½ each of red, orange & green bell pepper
¼ tsp cumin powder
¼ tsp garlic powder
1 avocado, pitted & sliced

FOR THE SALSA
2 tomatoes, chopped
½ white onion, finely chopped
2 jalapeno peppers, seeded & chopped
1/3 cup cilantro, chopped
2 tbsp fresh lime juice
1 tbsp gluten-free Mexican red chile sauce
Salt to taste

FOR THE LETTUCE DRESSING
1 tbsp olive oil
2 tbsp fresh lemon juice
1 tsp oregano
1 tsp gluten-free chipotle powder
½ tsp garlic powder
Salt to taste

Prep time: 15 mins • Cook time: 20 mins • Serves: 4

1 Combine all of the salsa ingredients and mix well. Refrigerate.

2 Over high heat, cook the black beans. Add the garlic salt, cumin powder and chili powder. Toss for 2-3 minutes. Add the pickled jalapenos and turn off the heat. Transfer to a bowl to cool.

3 Wash and heat the pan again. Add the dairy-free butter and corn, mixing until the corn is coated. Add the tajin and toss. Remove from heat and cool fully.

4 Heat the pan again, and add the bell pepper with ½ teaspoon avocado oil. Sauté for 2-3 minutes. Add the cumin powder and garlic powder. Stir for approximately 30 seconds, remove from the pan and set aside.

5 Pour the ingredients of the dressing over the lettuce and mix.

6 Combine the carnitas and the dairy-free cheese.

7 Preheat the oven to 350°F.

8 Heat a pan over high heat, add 1 tbsp of oil and pan fry the tortilla in the skillet. Cook for 30-40 seconds then flip, adding more oil if necessary. Cook until the tortilla is golden brown.

9 Place the hot tortilla in an oven-proof bowl. Push it down until it forms to the shape of the bowl. Repeat the process for all of the tortillas.

10 Place the bowls with the tortillas in the oven and bake for 8-9 minutes, or until crisp. Remove the tortillas from the bowl and cool.

11 Place the tortilla bowl on a plate. Add the lettuce, carnitas, black beans, corn, bell peppers, fresh jalapeno and sliced avocado. Serve with the salsa and dairy-free sour cream.

Pork Carnitas

Prep time: 10 mins
Cook time: 8 hours
Serves: 5-6

2 pounds boneless pork shoulder
½ tbsp lemon pepper
1 tbsp salt
1 small white onion, chopped
2 cloves garlic, minced
4-5 tbsp fresh orange juice
2 tbsp fresh lime juice
¼ cup cola soda
1 jalapeno
¾ tbsp dried oregano
1 tsp cumin powder
½ tsp chilli powder
¼ tsp onion powder
¼ tsp cinnamon powder
1 tbsp olive oil

1   Rinse the pork and pat it dry.

2   Mix the salt, lemon pepper, chili powder, oregano, cumin powder, onion powder and cinnamon powder.

3   Rub the pork with the spice mixture until it is thoroughly covered.

4   Place the pork in the slow cooker. Add the onion, garlic, jalapeno, lime juice, orange juice and cola soda. Close the lid and cook on high for 5-6 hours until the pork is tender. Remove the meat from the slow cooker and shred, using two forks to pull the meat apart. Keep the juice from the pork.

5   In a large pan, heat 1 tbsp of oil over high heat. Add the pork and drizzle with the leftover juice. Cook until the juices are evaporated and the bottoms and sides of the meat are crisp and brown. Flip the meat and briefly sear the other side. If you are using a smaller pan, do this step in multiple batches.

AUTHORS TIP
•   This pork is great in tacos, quesadillas, burritos and many other recipes!

FUSION

Sri Lankan Ramen Noodles

SPICE MIXTURE
2 tsp onion powder
1 tsp garlic powder
3 tbsp coriander seeds
2 red chillies
¼ tsp turmeric powder
2 tsp cumin
½ tsp lemon pepper
1 ½ tsp fenugreek seeds
½ tsp dry ginger powder
½ tsp garam masala
1 ½ tsp monk fruit sugar
½ tsp red chilli flakes
1 tbsp cornstarch
3 ½ tbsp dry mango powder
¼-½ tsp salt
½ tsp black pepper

NOODLES
4 packs gluten-free ramen noodles
8 garlic cloves, chopped lengthwise
10-12 asparagus, sliced into 1½
inch pieces
1 zucchini, sliced into 1½
inch pieces
6 baby carrots, chopped lengthwise
½ red and ½ yellow bell pepper, sliced
1 onion, thinly sliced
3-4 white shallots, chopped
¼ cabbage, thinly shredded
1 ½ nutiva coconut oil, butter flavor

Prep time: 15 mins • Cook time: 15 mins • Serves: 4

1 Roast the fenugreek seeds, cumin seeds, coriander seeds, red chili and black peppercorn in a pan at low heat for 1-2 minutes. Allow them to cool completely, then grind until they are powdered. Combine the remaining spice ingredients and grind once again. Store in an airtight container.

2 In a large pot, boil 6-7 cups of water and 1 tsp oil. As soon as the water begins to boil, add the ramen noodles. When they begin to soften, use a fork to separate the noodles. Cook over medium heat for an additional 2 minutes before straining and running under cold water to cool. The noodles should be al dente.

3 In a large wok, heat the coconut butter over high heat. Add the garlic and sauté until it is golden brown. Add the asparagus and cook for 1 minute. Add the zucchini and carrot strips. Sauté until tender, then add the onions and bell peppers.

4 Add the shallots, cabbage and 2 tbsp of the spice mixture. Stir fry for 1-2 minutes.

5 Add the boiled ramen and sauté until well mixed. Serve hot with chilies in vinegar.

Burmese Khow Suey

Prep time: 15 mins • Cook time: 15-20 mins • Serves: 2-3

KHOW SUEY SAUCE
2 tbsp coconut butter
(butter flavor) or avocado oil
½ cup onions, finely chopped
1 ½ tsp garlic
1 ½ tsp ginger
2 tbsp lemon grass paste
2 tbsp red Thai curry paste
¼ turmeric powder
1 ½ cup coconut milk
1 tbsp chickpea flour dissolved in ¼
cup vegetable stock or chicken stock
1 cup boiled vegetables (baby corn,
broccoli, carrot, french bean, zucchini,
button mushrooms)
½ red bell pepper
½ red onion, thinly sliced
Salt to taste
12 ounces chicken thighs, cut in small
bites
1 tbsp coconut butter flavor oil or
avocado oil

CONDIMENTS
1 ½ cups boiled rice noodles
1 ½ cups fried rice noodles
¼ cup garlic, deep fried
¾ cup sliced onions, deep fried
¼ cup spring onion, thinly sliced
¼ cup fried peanuts, crushed
2 tbsp fresh green chillies, finely
chopped
¼ cup cilantro, chopped
6 tbsp fresh lemon juice
Boiled eggs (optional), chopped

1 In a large wok heat 1tbsp oil. Add the red curry paste and sauté for 2-3 minutes over medium heat.

2 Add the chicken and cook until tender. Add the bell pepper, sliced onions and boiled vegetables. Sauté for another 4-5 minutes.

3 In another large pan, heat 1 ½ tbsp oil over medium heat. Add the garlic, ginger and onions. Sauté for 1-2 minutes. Add the lemon grass paste and turmeric and continue cooking until the onions are transparent. Cool and transfer to a blender. Blend into a paste.

4 Heat ½ tbsp oil in a large pot and add the the onion and turmeric paste. Sauté for 2-3 minutes. Add the chickpea paste and cook for another minute. Add the coconut milk and bring the mixture to a boil. Add salt, vegetables and chicken and red curry paste. Cook until the mixture comes to a boil, stirring occasionally.

5 Place the boiled noodles in 4 individual bowls and pour the khow suey sauce, vegetables and chicken over them. Top with the crispy noodles, fried onions, fried garlic, cilantro, lime, chili, spring onions and peanuts as desired. Serve immediately.

AUTHORS TIP
• To fry the noodles take the boiled noodles and spread them on a kitchen towel until the water is fully absorbed. Heat the wok with oil enough to fry. Fry small quantities of the noodles until they are golden brown. Remove the noodles from heat and set aside. The onions and garlic can be fried in the same oil.

Instapot Chicken Nihari

2 pounds skinless chicken thighs and breast
2 ½ cup oil for frying
¼ cup south asian multigrain gluten-free atta flour
4 cup low sodium chicken stock
4 cloves, ground
½ tsp fennel powder
½ tsp chilli powder
½ tsp coriander powder
½ tsp cumin powder
½ garlic powder
¼ tsp onion powder
2 ½ tbsp *Shan* nihari masala
1 tbsp coconut oil buttery flavor

CONDIMENTS

2 big onions, thinly sliced
15-20 garlic cloves, thinly chopped
1 ½ pieces ginger, julienned
¼ bunch cilantro, finely chopped
4-5 mild green chillies, chopped
4-5 green onions, chopped
6 tbsp fresh lemon juice
(or to taste)

Prep time: 40 mins • Cook time: 6.5 hours • Serves: 4

1   In a large wok, heat the oil and fry the chicken until it is golden brown. Remove the chicken, then in the same oil fry the onions and the garlic for the condiment.

2   Turn the Instapot on to the sauté setting. Add the chicken stock, half of the fried onions, chicken and all dry spices. When it begins to boil, turn off the Instapot and secure the lid. Set the pressure release to seal and the slow cook button. Set the timer for 6 hours, then naturally release.

3   Remove the bones from the chicken. Dissolve the flour in ½ cup water and pour in the chicken stew. Add the coconut oil. Cook on the stew setting for another 20 minutes until it begins to thicken.

4   Garnish with fried onions, fried garlic, cilantro, green onions, chilies and lemon juice in individual bowls. Serve immediately.

Tibetan Chicken with Steamed Bao

Prep time: 30 mins • Cook time: 40 mins • Serves: 4

½ tsp red chilli powder
2 pounds skinless boneless chicken thighs
8 ounces lotus stem
1 ½ white onion, chopped into cubes
1 red bell pepper, chopped into cubes
1 orange bell pepper, chopped into cubes
½ tsp garlic salt
½ tsp lemon pepper
Salt to taste
2 tbsp cornflour
1 tbsp rice flour
Pinch of baking powder
5 tbsp coconut oil or avocado oil

FOR THE SAUCE
8 dried red chillies, soaked in
2 tbsp distilled vinegar and
2 tbsp rice wine vinegar for at least 2-3 hours
8 garlic cloves
¼ onion powder
½ lemon salt
¼ garlic powder

1 Grind all of the sauce ingredients in the blender.

2 Marinate the chicken with salt and lemon pepper. Mix the corn flour, rice flour and baking powder. Sprinkle over the chicken and toss well.

3 Wash and clean the lotus stem and thinly slice.

4 Heat 2 tbsp of oil in a large wok and add the chicken pieces. Cook the chicken over high heat and continue saute till tender. Remove the chicken and set aside.

5 Heat 1 ½ tbsp oil and cook the lotus stem until golden brown. Remove and set aside to cool.

6 Heat the remaining oil in the wok and add the onion. Cook until translucent. Add the bell peppers and cook for 1-2 minutes. Add the blended sauce mixture. Cook until the vegetables are crisp yet tender.

7 Add the chicken, lotus stem, garlic salt and lemon pepper. Cook until completely mixed and the chicken is fully coated. Serve with Tibetan steamed bread.

Tibetan Steamed Bread

Prep time: 20 mins
Cook time: 15 mins
Serves: 12

2 cups rice flour
1 cup tapioca flour
1 cup potato starch
4 tsp xanthan gum
1 ½ tsp baking powder
2 tsp monk fruit sugar
10 gms instant yeast
½ tsp garlic salt
2 ½ tbsp coconut oil
(butter flavor) or 1 tsp olive oil mixed
with 2 tsp vegan butter
1 ¼ cup oat milk or almond milk

1   Sieve all of the flours and baking powder in a large bowl. Add the garlic salt and mix.

2   In the center of the bowl, make a well and then add the yeast and sugar.

3   Warm the milk and the oil. The milk should just be warmed, not hot. Pour this mixture over the yeast and set aside until you see bubbles.

4   Knead the dough very well for 5-7 minutes. Spray the dough lightly with olive oil, then cover the bowl in cling wrap. Let the dough rest for 3-4 hours.

5   Puncture the dough so it deflates, then knead the dough again. Divide the dough into 12 parts and roll into balls. Spray the dough balls with olive oil and let rest for 20 minutes.

6   Place the dough balls in a steamer with a cup of water, steam for 10 minutes. If the water evaporates, replenish it to complete the 10 minutes.

7   Remove the dough from heat and allow it to sit for 2-3 minutes or until fluffy and firm.

8   Serve with the Tibetan chicken or Tibetan black chickpeas.

Vietnamese Pork Pho

Prep time: 30 mins • Cook time: 8 hours
Makes 4 bowls

1 Lightly coat the onions and ginger with oil. Turn the broiler on to high heat. Place the onion and ginger on a baking sheet and set on the top rack. Broil for 7-10 minutes, or until the tops of the onion and ginger are slightly charred. Remove from heat and set aside.

2 Heat a pan on low and add the cinnamon sticks, coriander seeds, fennel seeds, star anise, cloves and cardamom. Roast until fragrant.

3 In a crockpot, add the pork chops and broth and bring to a boil. Add the charred onions, charred ginger and roasted dry spices. Cook on low for 8 hours.

4 Remove the meat from the crock pot and strain the spices. Keep the broth.

5 Separate the meat from the bone and set aside.

6 Add the fish sauce and sugar to the broth and bring to a boil.

7 Cook the noodles according to the package instructions and set aside.

8 Add the rice noodles to individual bowls. Pour the hot broth over the noodles. Add the shredded meat, green onions, herbs, sprout and chili garnish.

9 Add a squeeze of lime juice to each bowl and serve immediately.

BROTH

2 lbs pork chops
1 medium yellow onion, halved
3 inch piece ginger, sliced horizontally
5 star anise
4 garlic cloves
3 cinnamon sticks
3 green cardamom pods
1 tsp fennel seeds
1-1 ½ tbsp coriander seeds
8 cups low sodium chicken broth
½-¾ tbsp monk fruit sugar
2 tbsp fish sauce
Salt to taste

SOUP

8 ounces thin rice noodles
Cilantro
Mint
Thai basil
Green onions, sliced lengthwise
Lime wedges
Fresh red chilli, thinly sliced
¼ cup onion, thinly sliced
Bean sprouts

DESSERT

Banoffee Pie

Prep time: 45 mins • Serves: 10

3 cups dates
2 cups walnuts
1 cup coconut cream
400 ml coconut milk
(refrigerated overnight)
¼ cup almond butter
2 bananas
3 tbsp granulated monk fruit sugar

1 Add the walnuts and 1 cup dates to a food processor and blend until it becomes a dough like consistency. In a pie dish, push the dough evenly to form a crust and freeze for one hour.

2 Heat the remaining 2 cups of dates in the microwave for 45 seconds. Add to the food processor and blend until it begins sticking to the sides of the food processor. Add the coconut cream and almond butter to the food processor. Blend until it reaches a caramel like consistency. Smooth over the top of the pie base.

3 Chop the bananas into half inch pieces and layer on top of the date mixture.

4 Open the chilled coconut milk and scoop out the layer of cream on top. In a large bowl, mix the cream for 8-10 minutes, adding the sugar in small increments every 2 minutes.

5 Layer the cream over the bananas, making sure to cover them evenly. Chill for at least 2 hours in the freezer.

6 Move the pie to the fridge 30 minutes before serving. Garnish with thinly sliced bananas and chocolate shavings.

Prep time: 5 mins
Cook time: 25 mins
Serves: 6-8

1 cup gluten-free multigrain atta (flour)
1 cup powdered jaggery
1 cup coconut oil, butter flavor
3 ¼ cups water

Delicious Indian Halwa

1   In a saucepan over high heat mix powdered jaggery and water until completely dissolved, and it becomes a brown solution. Bring it to a boil then turn the flame off.

2   In a heavy wok over a low flame, heat the coconut oil. Once melted, add the gluten-free atta. Stir until there are no lumps remaining. Continue cooking the atta for 13-15 minutes constantly stirring. The flour mixture will turn a light mocha color and become fragrant.

3   Add the jaggery mixture to the flour mixture slowly, continuing to stir continuously. The mixture may bubble and will begin to thicken, but do not stop stirring. When you have reached a pudding like consistency, turn off the flame and serve immediately.

Microwave Chocolate Cake in a Mug

Prep time: 5 mins
Cook time: 2 mins • Serves: 1

4 tbsp almond flour
1 egg
4 tbsp chocolate chips
3 tbsp vegan butter or olive oil
½ tsp baking soda
½ tsp baking powder
1 tbsp coconut cream
Strawberries
½ banana

1 In a large mug, melt the butter and ¾ of the chocolate chips in the microwave for 30 seconds. Remove the mug from the microwave and stir with a fork until it becomes smooth.

2 Add the egg and coconut cream, and mix again. Add the almond flour, baking soda and baking powder. Mix until fully combined. Add the rest of the chocolate chips and mix.

3 Microwave for 1 ½ minutes. Keep an eye on it and stop the microwave if it begins to overflow. Insert a toothpick all the way to the bottom. If the batter sticks to the toothpick, continue to microwave in 30 second increments until the toothpick comes out clean.

4 Let the mug sit for 3 minutes to cool.

5 Serve with chopped strawberries and bananas.

Mini Key Lime Pie

Prep time: 25 mins
Serves: 6

1 cup cashews, soaked overnight
¾ cup coconut cream, refrigerated overnight
1 can 400 ml coconut milk
¼ cup melted coconut oil, butter flavor
½ cup lime juice
1/3 cup monk fruit sugar
1/3 cup water
¼ cup lime zest

1 Soak the cashews for at least 4 hours or overnight. Leave the can of coconut milk in the fridge overnight as well.

2 To make the simple syrup: In a small pan, bring water to a simmer. Add the monk sugar and stir until dissolved. Remove from heat and set aside.

3 Strain the cashews, add them to a food processor and blend until smooth. Add the simple syrup while the cashews are still warm and blend again. Add the coconut cream, coconut oil, lime zest and lemon juice. Blend.

4 Divide the mixture between 6 small glass bowls and freeze for 2 hours.

5 Open the coconut milk and scoop out the layer of cream at the top. Add the cream to a large bowl and whip for 8-10 minutes, adding sugar every 2 minutes. Spoon over the key lime pies and freeze overnight.

6 Remove the pies from the freezer 30 minutes before serving and garnish with lime zest and lime wedges.

Lemon & Coconut Mousse with Mango

Prep time: 10 mins
Cook time: 5 mins
Serves: 6-8

800 ml coconut cream
1 ¾ tbsp gelatine powder
4 tbsp hot water
5 tbsp honey
1/3 cup freshly squeezed lemon juice
1 ½ tsp vanilla extract
1 tbsp lemon zest
Mango, chopped into cubes

1 In a large bowl, combine the coconut cream, lemon zest and vanilla extract. Set aside.

2 In a small bowl, add the water and slowly add the gelatin while whisking with a fork. Set aside for 5 minutes until spongy.

3 Fill a large bowl with hot water. Set the smaller bowl with the gelatin inside it and stir until the gelatin is dissolved. Remove the smaller bowl and cool, then add honey and lemon juice.

4 Using an electric beater, whisk the coconut cream on low speed. Slowly add the gelatin mixture until combined.

5 Pour the lemon mousse mixture into individual glasses and place in the fridge to set overnight.

6 Top with chopped mango and serve.

AUTHORS TIP
• Do not boil the gelatin as it will become stringy.

As a self-proclaimed foodie the idea of completely cutting dairy and gluten out of my diet was terrifying. And yet, my motivation to manage and control the negative side affects of my PCOS outweighed my trepidation about limiting my diet so drastically. I was determined to make choices that would make my body feel good, without losing my love for food, and so this book was born. It is full of mouth watering recipes, and I hope that it will help you rediscover the joys of good food that also makes your body feel good. Enjoy!

Suhani Sethi